START DREAMING!

"Are you disappointed, discouraged, and discontented with your present level of success? Are you secretly dissatisfied with your present status? Do you want to become a better and more beautiful person than you are today? Would you like to be able to really learn how to be proud of yourself and still not lose genuine humility? Then start dreaming! It's possible! You can become the person you've always wanted to be!"

—Robert H. Schuller

Also by Robert H. Schuller from Jove

MOVE AHEAD WITH POSSIBILITY THINKING
PEACE OF MIND THROUGH POSSIBILITY THINKING
THE PEAK TO PEEK PRINCIPLE
POWER IDEAS FOR A HAPPY FAMILY
SELF-LOVE

YOU CAN BECOME THE PERSON YOU WANT TO BE

Robert H. Schuller

A JOVE BOOK

This Jove book contains the complete
text of the original hardcover edition.
It has been completely reset in a typeface
designed for easy reading, and was printed
from new film.

YOU CAN BECOME THE PERSON YOU WANT TO BE

A Jove Book / published by arrangement with
Hawthorn Books, Inc.

PRINTING HISTORY
Hawthorn Books edition published 1973

Six previous paperback printings
Jove edition / November 1978
Sixteenth printing / August 1983

All rights reserved.
Copyright © 1973 by Robert H. Schuller
This book may not be reproduced in whole
or in part, by mimeograph or any other means,
without permission. For information address:
Hawthorn Books, Inc., 2 Park Avenue,
New York, New York 10016.

ISBN: 0-515-07417-9

Library of Congress Catalog Card Number: 72-7783

Jove books are published by The Berkley Publishing Group,
200 Madison Avenue, New York, N.Y. 10016.
The words "A JOVE BOOK" and the "J" with sunburst
are trademarks belonging to Jove Publications, Inc.

PRINTED IN THE UNITED STATES OF AMERICA

ACKNOWLEDGMENTS

Appreciation is expressed to the *Hour of Power* for permission to reprint the Possibility Thinker creed. Certain portions of this book were originally published by the *Hour of Power* under the title *Become a Possibility Thinker Now*.

Dedicated to
my good friend
Norman Vincent Peale
who, perhaps more than any
other minister of our
century, has taught millions
of people to
believe that they could become
the persons God intended them
to be

Contents

Introduction: It's Possible!   11

1
You Can Become the Person You Want to Be   15

2
Set Your Goals and Let Them Lift You   24

3
Problem-Solving Principles That Work   37

4
Self-Confidence—Get It! Use It! Keep It!   47

5
Play the Possibility Thinking Game—And Win!   62

6
Now—Wipe Out Fear of Failure and Move Ahead   74

7
Winning Starts With Beginning   86

8
Enthusiasm—This Power Will Put You in Orbit!   101

9
Keep Charged Up—With a Positive Mental Attitude!   110

10
Never Give Up   124

11
Prayer + Possibility Thinking = Success   140

12
Here Is the Person You Really Want to Be   152

INTRODUCTION: IT'S POSSIBLE!

Is it possible for an overweight fifty-nine-year-old man who has never been athletic and who looks and feels older than his years—is it possible for such a man to become a record-breaking long-distance runner?

Is it possible for a high school girl whose grades in chemistry were never better than D to go on to college and get top marks in the toughest courses in organic chemistry?

Can a cerebral palsied quadriplegic learn to walk? Can a near-high-school dropout become one of the world's leading brain surgeons? Is it possible for a cast-off Negro orphan to become a prominent MD?

Many people, especially those who think negatively, would say that all of these things are impossible. But I know the people who have had these seemingly miraculous changes in their lives and how they accomplished them.

Think of this: She's barely twenty years old. She speaks only Spanish when she arrives in Los Angeles with seven dollars in her pocket. She saves four hundred dollars, starts a taco business, turns it into a multimillion-dollar operation, and becomes treasurer of the United States of America! Is this possible? Well, it happened! (She is Romana Bañuelos.)

Is it possible to find joy and happiness when the person you've loved more than life is taken away from you? "I wanted to die when my husband died. There was no glimmer of desire to go on, until God gave me the miracle of new life," said Doris Day. Then she made a new start.

Revive Your Dreams—Now!

Have you had a dream that once lived in your mind only to die? Have you tried one career and another and failed until you've reached the conclusion that your dream is unrealistic and hopeless? Are you disappointed, discouraged, and discontented with your level of success? Are you secretly dissatisfied with your present status? Do you want to become a better and more beautiful person than you are today? Would you like to be able to really learn how to be proud of yourself and still not lose genuine humility? Then start dreaming! It's possible! You can become the person you've always wanted to be!

How? There is a KEY—there is a SECRET—there is a WAY—to turn impossible dreams into fantastic accomplishments. I call it *Possibility Thinking*. Some call it faith. Jesus said, "If you have faith as a grain of mustard seed you can say to your mountain 'move'. And nothing will be impossible to you!"

Here's how it works. When a person begins to believe it just might be possible, somehow, someway, somewhere, someday—then in that magic moment of Possibility Thinking three miracles occur: (1) Opportunity-spotting brain cells activate! (2) Problem-solving brain cells come to life. (3) Determination-energizing chemicals are released into the blood stream! I promise you it really works if you diligently work at it!

I Offer You a Ladder

In front of you now is an invisible ladder. It rises higher and higher. Take the first step. Put your hands on the rung. Put your right foot on the first step. Good. You are starting to rise. You will become the person you want to be!

The higher you climb—the farther you'll see! Self-confidence will begin to surge within you. Unbelievable surprises await you at the top of that ladder. *Start today,* or you'll be like the man who prayed, "Oh God, spare me from the hell of seeing the great opportunities I missed because I lacked the faith to believe and begin."

Your conscious mind is like a dike holding back an ocean of unimaginable, undiscovered, undeveloped possibilities. All I ask you to do now is to put one tiny hole in that dike! You do that when you decide to give Possibility Thinking a real try!

1

YOU CAN BECOME THE PERSON YOU WANT TO BE

Do you sometimes have a depressed feeling that you haven't achieved as much as you should have? Do you occasionally see other persons with apparently less talent, intelligence, dedication, and skill passing you by?

Have you ever had a gnawing suspicion that there just might be a better life for you than you're living today? Is it possible, you wonder, that you're missing the mark and not getting your share? What's wrong? Who's to blame for your achievement level that remains too low on the scoreboard? If you had a dream die within you—who killed it? Whose fault is it that you haven't progressed farther—faster?

How Do You Start?

How do you start to become that person you want to be? First, by analyzing the negative forces that have been holding you back. Find the reasons for your inertia. You must place the blame where it properly belongs before you can correct the situation.

Have you ever played the game "Let's Pick Out the Villain"? If you've been taught, or are naturally inclined to place the blame on any one class or group or people who have a different creed or are of a different color than you, you are making a big mistake. There are too many other persons in the same position who are succeeding in spite of proud or prejudiced opposition.

Try again: "It's our capitalistic system." Wrong again. In spite of its faults, our free enterprise system—more than any other in the world—allows you the freedom to choose to try to become anything your heart desires.

"My parentage is inadequate. The blame is in my breeding." Ridiculous! You still have a brain with trillions of cells! It's an instrument of such incalculable capabilities that one engineer has estimated it would take a building several *acres* in size to house the computers that would match the dullest human brain! And at that, though you'd have the world's smartest man-made computer, it would still lack the self-input generating power that *every* human being possesses.

"The Establishment is putting and keeping me down." Sorry! That's a sweeping, negative generalization that would never stand up in the court of reality. The hundreds of thousands of disadvantaged people who are making great strides today in our Establishment turn this argument into an excuse. Remember: *You'll never successfully solve the problem until you correctly place the blame!* Ask yourself this question: If others—in worse straits than I—are making it WHY NOT I?

The real oppressive power in human society is *Impossibility Thinking*. And the truly oppressed person is the *Impossibility Thinker*.

An Impossibility Thinker is a person who, when he sees something wrong with an idea, a plan, an organization, an institution, a tradition, or a person, born or unborn, votes to abandon, abolish, or abort it!

A *Possibility Thinker*, liberated from perfectionism, knows that there's something wrong with every idea, plan, organization, institution, tradition, and person. "What's good about it?" he questions. "Is there any positive value in this suggestion?" he asks. If so, he then begins to divide and conquer. He assumes that there must be a way to separate, insulate, eliminate, or sublimate the negative aspect in the situation. He believes that if he persists in exhausting all possibilities he will discover or invent a way to isolate, activate, cultivate, and harvest the positive values. I call this *Sanctified Exploitation*.

A Possibility Thinker never votes no to any idea that holds some possibility for good. Before he votes yes to a problem-plagued positive possibility he may move to amend, modify, qualify, or delay, but *never* will he cast an unqualified no vote to any suggestion that has within it the seed of some possible positive good! Just because it's impossible is no reason to vote no to a potentially great idea.

Creativity starts when some Possibility Thinker challenges the problems in the positive idea that everyone knows is impossible. In other words, he never throws away the baby with the dirty water.

The Possibility Thinker will cast an unreserved negative vote only when the issue violates his moral, religious, and ethical value system.

You become your own tyrant when you surrender your will to the negative thoughts that you carelessly allow admittance into the sacred and unguarded areas of your mind! In that defenseless moment, and in that irresponsible action, you become your own oppressor. You—and no one else but YOU—have the power to receive, welcome, and nourish the dream-destroying, opportunity-abandoning, success-strangulating negative thoughts in your mind.

Of all the persons living on Planet Earth, there is only one person who has the power to cast the deciding vote to kill your dream. That person is YOU. *You* cast that death-sentencing vote to your dream when *you* decide to quit hoping, stop trying, and give up.

The Tiger Cage of Your Mind

You begin to live when you arouse and liberate your slumbering potentialities.

What is a tiger cage? A veteran of the Vietnam conflict answered that question before an audience of rapt listeners. For four years he was a prisoner of war held in a Viet Cong tiger cage. Because the communist guerrillas in South Vietnam were constantly on the move through the jungles, they kept their P.O.W.'s, not in fixed prison camps, but in small portable prisons that could be quickly picked up and moved. That's how the tiger cage was invented. Made from bamboo sticks, the little jails often averaged about five feet in length and approximately four feet wide, too small for a tall American to stretch out.

Year after year—up to six years in at least one case— American prisoners of war remained cramped, crowded, and confined in these portable prisons. "One night I succeeded in working one bamboo stick loose. That was all I needed to step out and I was free," the navy flier reported to his entranced listeners.

I looked at the faces of the members of the comfortable, well-to-do audience sitting in the plush ballroom of that California hotel and I saw not just an escaped navy flier but the faces of hundreds of people who were trapped themselves in tiger cages of their own making.

Imprisoned within every person's mind are vast possibilities that have never had the chance to be realized. No power on earth is greater than man's power to dream, visualize, and imagine. No human suffering is more tragic than to see human beings live—and finally die—without ever having released their imprisoned powers of a God-given creative imagination. From childhood, through adolescence, into adulthood, we allow a tiger cage to be built around our minds that constricts creative urges. This might explain why, as tests have shown, some children surpass top-flight business executives in solving creative brain-bending problems. The longer we live the more we tend to "lock in" our creative imagination.

To become the person you want to be, you must first loosen the bars in your mind. In this book you will learn how to work loose, pry loose, kick loose, and maneuver yourself free from the bars of your mental tiger cage.

Eliminate Fear of Failure

One big bar in the mental tiger cage is called *Fear of Failure*. Nothing blocks dynamic creativity more than such a fear. Why? Because a fear of failure is really a fear of embarrassment. The need for self-esteem is one of the deepest of all human needs. To expose our self-dignity to the hazard of public ridicule is a risk we instinctively avoid! Our inclination is to play it safe and avoid the possibility of a disgrace by not even trying.

Work this confining, negative concept loose from your thinking. Here's the way. Remember that not failure but low aim is the crime.

> Not to Win
> is
> Not a Sin!

To try to do something great and fail can be one of the greatest things you've ever done in your life! I am always pleased to meet people who dared try!

I've often thought I'd like to create a national award to be given away each year—an award entitled "The Most Glorious Failure of the Year Award." I would bestow it upon the man or woman, boy or girl, who tried courageously against overwhelming obstacles, and lost! The truth, of course, is such people are not failures at all! They are successes, with flying colors, as persons! For failure is not failure to meet your goal. Real failure is failure to reach as high as you possibly can. No man will ever truly know that he has succeeded until he experiences an apparent failure. The pole vaulter cannot be certain that he has jumped as high as he possibly can until he knocks the bar down! Keep raising your goals until you have a failure! Then and only then will you know that you have reached your peak. You have truly succeeded when you have seemingly failed.

Learn the Tricks of Problem Solving

Do you have a natural inclination to allow problems to stop you from dreaming? Then there is another imprisoning bar in your mind that will have to be removed. It is absolutely essential that you develop a sensible, workable philosophy for solving problems.

> **Solve Your Problems
> or
> Your Problems Will
> Dissolve You**

If only one truth in this book really grips you, let it be this one: Never surrender the leadership of your life to problems whether they are real or imaginary. Possibility Thinkers are motivated by problems. They know that every problem is an opportunity to be creative. Problems stop negative thinkers; problems start Possibility Thinkers! Problems paralyze impossibility thinkers. Problems mobilize Possibility Thinkers. Resolve now—never to let problems keep you from dreaming! Simply assume that if you're clever enough to imagine a problem you're clever enough to discover a solution! Remember: If your imagination conjures up problems as quickly as it creates opportunities, that's good! It may be God's way of testing you to see if you have faith enough to begin. If you visualize great obstacle surrounded possibilities, that's wonderful! This gives God a chance to perform some miracles! Millions of miracles are happening every day. Why not be bold enough to claim your share?

The Tyranny of Unpleasant Memories

Is the tyranny of unpleasant memories the bar in the tiger cage of your mind? Do old hurts and disappointments, set-backs, or previous rejections haunt you? You really don't have to surrender your future to these negative forces. Let these unpleasant memories die. Do not allow these ghosts to sit in the driver's seat of your mind.

Let your dreams, not your regrets, take command of your life. Liberate your imprisoned creative imagination from the tyranny of depressing recollections. Today is the beginning of a new adventure. Imagine the exciting things that could happen to you tomorrow. Before long you'll have a new hobby of collecting happy memories! There'll be one more loose bar in your tiger cage! Fear not that if you move ahead you'll have more bad experiences. Fear, rather, that if you don't try again you'll miss your great chance to start having a really happy life!

Build A Powerful Self-Confidence

Another bar in the tiger cage that stultifies our creativity is lack of self-confidence. If you assume that you are inferior, you will suffer a disastrous failure. If you assume problems will block and defeat you; that if you try you'll only get hurt again, you have already fashioned another oppressive concept in your mind: "I can't do it! It won't work for me." A negative self-image will become another bar in the tiger cage of your mind.

Break this binding chain with powerful, God-filled affirmations:

"If God be for me who can be against me?"

"I can do all things through Christ who strengthens me."

"All things are possible to me if I will believe."

I broke the chain of inferiority feelings within myself and acquired self-confidence through two Bible verses.

"Be confident in this one thing that God who has begun a good work in you (He has been giving you the will, the hope, the dream, the desire) will complete it!" (Phil 1:6) (He will give you the secret, the strength, and the skill to succeed!)

"For it is God working in you, giving you the will and the power to achieve His Purposes." (Phil. 2:13)

Memorize, and saturate your thinking with these Bible verses.

A tourist walked down a pier and watched a fisherman pull in a large fish, measure it, and throw it back. He caught a second fish, smaller this time, he measured it, and put it in his bucket. Oddly, all the large fish that he caught that measured ten inches or more he discarded. All fish smaller than ten inches he kept. Puzzled, the curious onlooker questioned, "Pardon me, but why do you keep the little ones and throw the big ones away?" The old fellow looked up and without blinking an eye said, "Why, because my frying pan measures only ten inches across!"

Foolish? Of course. But no more so than when you throw away the biggest ideas and the most beautiful dreams that come into your mind simply because your experience is too limited, your self-confidence too undeveloped to enable you to grab hold of the big opportunities God sends your way!

Start growing now. Think big. Big things happen to big-thinking people. Nothing big happens to little-thinking people.

You can become the person you want to be. It's possible. You'll discover this as you begin to break free from the tiger cage of impossibility thinking.

Join in a grand adventure of discovering the beautiful life God has been planning for you. Join the exciting crowd of energetic, enthusiastic, youthful possibility thinkers.

Ten Commandments For Possibility Thinkers

There are ten rules you must follow as you read these pages. Ignore them and you will deprive yourself of immeasurable excitement, achievement, and success. I call these principles the ten commandments for possibility thinkers. It is imperative that you acquaint yourself with them now—at the outset—before you ever try to expand your thinking.

1. You will never vote no to any idea because "It's impossible."

2. You will never block a helpful thought because it entails problems, or wait to begin until you find a solution to every problem.

3. You will never oppose a possibility because you've never done it and can't imagine how it could be done.

4. You will never obstruct a plan because it runs a risk of failure.

5. You will never cooperate in defeating a potentially good suggestion because you can see something wrong with it.

6. You will never squelch a creative idea because no one else has ever succeeded in perfecting it.

7. You will never declare any constructive concept to be impossible because you lack the time, money, brains, energy, talent, or skill to exploit it.

8. You will never discard a plan or a project just because it's imperfect.

9. You will never resist a proposal because you didn't think of it, you won't get the credit, you won't personally benefit from it, or you may not live to see and enjoy it.

10. You will never quit because you've reached the end of the rope. Tie a knot and hang on.

Now, start dreaming! Be sure to make your dreams big enough for God to fit in!

2

SET YOUR GOALS
AND LET THEM LIFT YOU

What goals would you be setting for yourself if you knew you could not fail?

What dreams would you have on the drawing board if you had unlimited financial resources?

What plans would you be making if you had thirty years to carry them out?

What projects would you be launching if you had the wisdom to solve any problem and the power to sweep all obstacles out of your way?

What exciting work would you be engaged in today if you could acquire the skill to sell your ideas to powerful people?

What role should you play in the drama of human life? Clarify your role before you set your goal or you'll encounter confusion and frustration. Conflict in inter-personal relations is too often the result of a misinterpretation by the involved persons of the roles each should be playing. Here's a simple formula for success Role▶ Goal + Toll = SUCCESS. Define your role; then, and then only, get set to establish your goal. Be prepared to pay the price in terms of time, money, energy and credit-sharing, and you'll succeed.

Now go back to the opening of this chapter and re-think, slowly and carefully, these big questions. Do not be held back by past failures. When the sun rises tomorrow, the light of the new day will illuminate an open door that beckons you to enter a new world called The Land of Beginning Again! Prepare for that fantastic experience by rereading those opening questions.

Stretch your mind before you sketch your goals. An athlete doesn't step into the arena without doing his warm-up exercises. Re-read the above questions and you will find your creative imagination will begin to focus on exciting possibilities!

Now you're ready to review, reevaluate, revise, and redesign your life's goals.

Success or failure starts right here. Set low goals—and achievements will be low. Your goal setting—perhaps more than any other factor in life—will determine whether or not you amount to what you should have amounted to in life.

> Aim at Nothing And You'll Succeed

Goal setting—then—there's where success starts or failure begins.

In the Institute for Successful Church Leadership, which I conduct in Garden Grove, California, we aim to turn ministers and church leaders into dynamic Positive Thinkers. So we ask the pastors to write out their five-, ten-, fifteen-, and twenty-year goals. Of the more than two thousand graduates only once have I seen goals that caused me to say, "They're unrealistic—too high! Too fast!" Almost always the goals the Leadership Institute students set are too low and not too slow!

Are there universal principles that we can use to set our goals in our personal and professional lives? There are indeed. Let me share them with you.

Consider the Talents You Have

Possibility Thinkers begin in their goal setting by examining realistically their God-given talents.

Make a list of all the things you think you do well and then make a list of those things you'd like to do well. Analyze both lists.

Discover the undiscovered talents within you but think realistically. They are there! Look for them.

Jim Poppen was an underachiever in high school. Teachers could easily have misjudged him to be only average, or below average, in intelligence and talent. Now, in retrospect, we know that he didn't lack talent—he only lacked motivation which was the result of an absence of challenging goals. When he expressed a vague interest in medicine his farmer father made arrangements for Jim to get into a school where this inclination could be tested. Jim Poppen's cousin, a member of my church staff, says, "No one would ever have bet a thin dime that he'd amount to anything."

The young fellow returned home for Christmas vacation. It was a cold, dark night in the Michigan country home. In the stillness of midnight the father awoke hearing odd sounds coming out of the pitch black kitchen. Stealthily he groped his way out of his bedroom, through the kitchen door, flipped on a light, and saw his young son sprawled on the floor enmeshed in a crazy network of ropes tied to the rickety legs of the old kitchen chairs. "My son has flipped! His mind can't stand the strain of study," was his father's first reaction. Before he could speak, Jim barked out orders, "Put the lights off, Dad! In school last month I discovered the human brain. I'm going to be a brain surgeon. So I've got to learn to tie knots in the dark." But could the thick fingers of a farmer's son, and the undisciplined mind of a mediocre student dredge up the talent to make it? Well, he did!

Some years ago I was driving to my office when the newscaster broke the horrible news:

> Presidential candidate Robert Kennedy has been shot through the head. His condition is grave at this moment as he lies in a Los Angeles hospital. Further details are lacking. However, it has been learned that the Kennedy family has summoned the world-famed brain surgeon from Boston, Massachusetts, Dr. James Poppen, who is now flying to the West Coast.

Only God knows what slumbering talents are waiting to be aroused within your undiscovered self! Whatever you do, always let your future desires, and never your past defeats, set your goals for you!

A friend of mine started studying the piano seriously at the age of sixty. Two years later, she was good enough to be giving lessons to little children. Because she is such a sweet, pleasant, beautiful soul, the children love her and she is a success. "Don't you have to be very skilled before you can teach others?" I asked her. "Not really," she answered, "just better than my students! And I only take beginners—and stay a step ahead of them!"

Explore your latent interests. Uncover untapped talent. Remember this: The fact that there are more "talented" people who are failures and more "untalented people" who are successes proves that talent is not the most essential ingredient for obtaining what you want or being the person you want to be.

Consider Your God-given Drive

Again and again, first prizes don't go to the most talented man—again and again the man who wins is the one who is sure that he can! A powerful fact is this: *A great drive, a powerful determination, a consuming desire, will easily compensate for little or limited talent.*

By the standard of the Impossibility Thinker, the man who booted the longest field goal in the history of pro football, couldn't do it. But no one told him that, and he did the impossible. Most football fans know his name, Tom Demsey. He was born with only half a right foot and a deformed right arm and hand. Even though he successfully overcame his handicap and played outstanding football in high school and college, he was turned down by the professional teams. They said, "You are not professional material." He refused to accept that. He explains, "I have never learned to give up. So many times in life and in sports, I have seen things turn around because someone has persevered, someone has kept faith." He adds this word of testimony about his own family: "My parents are blessed with this kind of faith." Finally he was taken as a player by the New Orleans Saints.

Demsey's record field goal decided a very close game between the Detroit Lions and the Saints. Just when it seemed as though the Saints had victory in their grasp, and with only eleven seconds left in the game, the Lions' kicker booted a field goal from 18 yards out and put them ahead 17-16. It looked like the game was over. In two plays the Saints took the kickoff back to their own 45 yard line. Now

there were only two seconds left. The coach sent Tom into
the game to attempt the longest field goal ever made. It
would take a 63 yard kick to send the ball from the point
of his toe across the bar between the uprights. The longest
field goal that had ever been kicked in professional football
up to that time had been 56 yards. Tom was so far from
the goal posts that even though he was sure when he made
contact with the ball that it was going straight, he wasn't
sure that it had crossed the bar until the official underneath
raised his arms to signal a score. The Saints had won. Tom
heard someone say after the game, "Unbelievable." He just
smiled, for seldom had his coaches talked to him in nega-
tives. As Tom tells it, "They were always so busy encourag-
ing me they simply forgot to tell me what I couldn't do!"

One of the most baffling questions waiting to be respon-
sibly answered by psychological researchers today is whether an all-consuming drive can create talent where talent
presumably does not exist. There is mounting evidence that
this may indeed be true. John Stewart, the New York City
Opera Company star, was advised by "experts" that his
voice just "isn't the instrument of a professional singer."
He was advised to give up his desire to perform and prepare instead to teach music. No one today doubts that he
has talent. It appears that talent is the description given by
an approving public to a disciplined, determined, dedicated, and undefeatable dreamer who is driven by an all-
consuming desire to succeed.

Does a mentally retarded Mongoloid have the natural
talent to become educable? Of course not! Or so experts
have always agreed. Yet I visited the mentally retarded section of the public school in Mitchell, South Dakota, and
saw twelve youngsters fired up with an incredible drive to
learn.

Three weeks prior, in a visit to a similar school in California, the principal, specially trained for teaching the
Down's Syndrome children, told me, "These children do
not have the ability to learn to read or write. However, we
do teach them the meaning of a few pictures like danger
and exit and men and women." I was impressed with that
degree of learning until the teacher in South Dakota had
her class read *whole sentences!* "We haven't begun to dis-

cover how much talent these youngsters have," she reported, her eyes flashing with excitement. "And confidentially," she spoke softly, pointing to one of the better readers with slanted eyes, "that little girl has an IQ of only forty-one."

Dr. Irving Stone, an eminent psychologist specializing in working with the severely mentally retarded children in Fairview State Hospital in Costa Mesa, California, listened intently as I gave the above account. "It's so true," the brilliant doctor enthused, "we have just come to the conclusion that as far as the learning ability of these children is concerned our official policy must change to—anything is possible!" Then, with a hint of humble professional penitence, he added, "We now know that we have been limiting these persons by our own lack of belief in that vast unfathomed potential lying dormant in the retarded mind. It now appears that our minds have been retarded in imagining what they can accomplish if they are properly motivated, inspired, and trained."

Consider the Challenges That Confront You

Rediscover the universal principle that every problem is an opportunity! Difficulties often become challenges to make you a bigger, broader, better, or more beautiful person than ever before.

In my book, *Move Ahead with Possibility Thinking*, the story of Norm and Sarah Rassmussen illustrated this point. When their fifth child was born a Mongoloid, they turned their problem into a project and took four other Mongoloid foster children into their home. Now there's a new chapter to their story. Norm, an aerospace engineer, was laid off during a period of industrial personnel cutbacks. Instead of looking at his unemployment as a problem, he looked at it as an opportunity. Holding that attitude, he developed an idea. He and Sarah began operating a full-time foster home center for Mongoloid children!

Do you need help in setting personal goals? Consider the challenging spot you're in right now. If you are in the hospital, your goal today may be to raise an arm, tomorrow to raise a leg, next you'll aim at rolling over on your side, then getting up and walking to the bathroom, then sitting up in a chair and then, one day, walking in the hallway—home! Inch by inch, anything's a cinch!

Remember this: In setting your goals, bloom where you are planted.

Your mental attitude toward the spot you're in at any moment is all important. If you think it's impossible, then your biggest problem is *you!* If you "think possibilities," you'll realize that every difficulty is a call to some personal triumph.

When you have invented a solution to a difficult problem or adjusted to a trying situation, you will know the high and happy feeling that comes when you experience personal triumph.

Once, while I was driving through the desert, the tire on my car went flat. I jacked up the rear end of the car and just managed to get the tire off when the jack broke and the car fell on its axle. I was stranded. No way now to raise the car.

"Wait a minute! Let's dig a hole," my wife suggested. So we did. Fortunately, I was off the pavement and on the shoulder. Indeed it was about as hard as cement. But with the tire wrench I chipped away! Stone by stone, pebble by pebble, I labored until I had dug a hole deep enough to take the flat tire off and drop the spare tire into—and onto the waiting bolts! Did I ever feel the exhilaration of a personal triumph! Every problem can become a personal triumph, making life a real adventure from beginning to end!

> If you never challenge personal problems,
> you'll never be able to taste the exhilaration of
> a Personal Triumph!

Remember: Triumph is made up of two words: TRY and UMPH.

Consider the Values You Live By

I was shocked to learn that an ex-convict read my book on Possibility Thinking and was inspired to plot an unbelievable holdup! He was thinking possibilities, but the wrong kind.

What is all important in setting goals is to consider the

SET YOUR GOALS AND LET THEM LIFT YOU 31

value system you choose to live by. If money or material objects are your highest values, the questions you ask before you set your goals will be:

"How much will it cost?"
"How much money will I make?"
"What are the fringe benefits?"

If security is your chief value, you'll ask these questions before you set your goals:

"Can I be sure of success?"
"Is it risky?"
"Is there a possibility of failure?"

If Christ's Spirit lives within you, then you'll live by the *Service Value System*, which is placing enormous value on unselfishly serving your fellow man and the first questions you'll raise in your goal setting will be:

"Will this help people who are hurting?"
"Will this make me into a more beautiful person?"
"Will this bring the best out of me—or the worst?"
"Will this be a chance to prove my faith in a big God?"

Man may not always make his goals, but
his goals will always make the man.

If you are deeply committed to a value system, major decisions will be made swiftly and confidently. As a churchman I serve as the chairman of the board of three separate church-affiliated corporations. Anytime a positive idea is suggested we ask these three questions: Would it be a great thing to do for God? Would it help people who are hurting? Is anybody else doing anything about it?

If the answer to the first two questions is yes and the answer to the third is no, the decision is made. It must be done! We resolve to do it and trust we will solve the problems as they arise. We allow no precious time or priceless creative mental energy to be wasted in delay, debate, and decision making. We make our decision. We will either do it ourselves—or spearhead a drive, or form a new organization, or put together a new corporation, or appoint a projects committee to get the ball rolling! Be confident! If you make a wrong decision it simply means you must make another decision.

On a tour for the air force in the Far East I heard about

a dynamic general who noted Vietnam civilians suffering from lack of medical facilities and asked why nothing was being done to relieve their misery. He was told, "It's an impossible situation." He called his immediate subordinate and ordered: "I want you to call together the best minds in our outfit to dream up a solution to this problem. I don't want you to spend one minute deciding whether it can or should be done. I am ordering you to spend every minute and every ounce of mental energy dreaming up all of the possible ways in which we *can* get a hospital *built* and supplied—NOW!"

The subordinate who took the command said, "It was absolutely amazing how fast and furious the creative ideas flowed when we got together! In sixty days the medical facility was fully operational."

Consider What Resources Are Available

Consider the resources that are available in the world today. Do not consider the resources you have on hand. Consider the resources that are available in the world!

Because you do not have the time, talent, money, brains, skill, energy, or organization is no excuse for not trying if your cause is right! Brain power, money power, energy power, is abundant in the world and gravitates to Big Ideas and Big Thinking persons like flecks of steel gravitate to a magnet.

Time may be your crucial consideration. But it's possible to buy time in many cases. Perhaps you should hire more people to do the job faster. You can't afford to? Then, I say you have a money problem, not a time problem. Money problems are generally much easier to solve!

Time is a major resource to consider in goal setting. I started the Garden Grove Community Church when I was twenty-eight years old. "I'll spend forty years here," I dreamed, and you can be sure that attitude caused me to enlarge my dream enormously!

A word of special warning to the senior citizen: Don't underestimate the time you still may have left! Following a Possibility Thinking lecture on a Pacific cruise ship, an enthusiastic listener told me, "I wish I had heard that thirty years ago. I could have died a millionaire." I guessed his age at about fifty-seven. "How old are you?" I asked. "Sixty-eight," he answered, smiling. "Then you're not too old to begin!" I challenged. "You look so young and healthy you just might live to be ninety-eight—that's thirty years away! Start today or twenty years from now you'll be moaning, 'Why didn't I start twenty years ago when I was still young.'"

If you are so advanced in years that you cannot reasonably imagine yourself living long enough to complete your dream, then what? Consider not the time resources God has given you—but consider the time resources God has! My dad planted a new apple orchard when he was nearly eighty because he knew that God would provide the time to bring the trees to full fruitfulness for someone, someday, to enjoy!

The truth is we all have unbelievable, untapped resources within ourselves this very moment! A friend of mine saw a four-stack file cabinet fall on his small child who was attempting to climb it. Instantly the father leaped to his feet and lifted the four-hundred pound cabinet, freeing his injured son. "I don't know where the energy and strength came from," he said.

God has unlimited resources that He can make available to people who think big and believe deeply.

Consider The Opportunities Around You

Finally, if you are living in the United States of America you have enormous freedom to choose almost any career your heart desires. "Think opportunities" and set your goals.

A young eighteen-year-old boy said to me recently, "I'd love to spend my life making a million dollars and die giving it away to the great causes that need money desperately. But I can't realistically imagine ever succeeding."

"Can you believe that you might possibly live to the age of seventy-eight?" I asked. "Yes, I can," he answered. "Then I can show you how you can be a millionaire in your lifetime," I promised. "Simply exercise Possibility Thinking and plan your life. Here's *how* you can do it: Work—earn—and save fifteen hundred dollars next year. Increase this to an average of two thousand dollars a year for the next twenty years. At the age of thirty-eight you'll have a savings account of forty thousand dollars. Now invest this at eight percent interest. Allow the interest to compound annually. Form a nonprofit corporation to hold this money. And without adding any additional savings your forty thousand dollars will grow into one million dollars in forty years! At the age of seventy-eight you'll have a million dollars to give away! That's a mathematical fact." He was stunned! "I'll do it," he said. I believe he really will!

A young boy approached a wealthy contractor standing on the sidewalk surveying the tall office structure he was building. "Tell me, sir," the boy asked, "how can I be successful like you when I grow up?" The gray-haired builder smiled kindly then spoke in the tough language of his trade, "Easy son. Buy a red shirt and work like crazy." Knowing that the youngster didn't understand, the wealthy builder of skyscrapers explained, pointing to the skeleton of his rising new structure. "See all those men up there? See that man in the red shirt? I don't even know his name. But I've been noticing how hard he works. One of these days I'm going to need a new superintendent. I'll go to that fellow and say—'Hey you in the red shirt—come here!' He'll get the big opportunity!"

Remember: Most people fail, not because they lack talent, money, or opportunity; they fail because they never really planned to succeed. Plan your future because you have to live there!

**If You Fail to Plan,
You Are Planning to
Fail**

In 1955 I planned to start a new church. With five hundred dollars, my wife as a member, and the use of a drive-in theater as a meeting place, we started. I drew a mental picture of the church I hoped to build—gardens, flowers, people, staff. Today, visitors stroll through the twenty-two-acre campus. They ride glass elevators to the Chapel in the Sky fifteen floors over the garden grounds. They're impressed.

They express disbelief. "I'm not impressed or surprised," I answer with complete honesty, adding, "after all—we planned it this way!"

Set definite goals. Write them out. Draw a picture. Imprint them into your subconscious through the video channel of your eye. Now affirm positively *out loud*, your hope for achievement. Visualize, then verbalize your goals. In so doing you are conditioning your subconscious through the audio, as well as the video imput channel of your body and mind. Repeat this mind-conditioning treatment daily and you will be instructing your subconscious to direct your life toward the realization of determined goals. Set a timetable to accomplish each phase, to create the pressure upon yourself to begin, and continue to progress steadily toward your goal. It is important that you set a definite time limit by which each phase must be accomplished. Otherwise, procrastination and delay will pilot your project, and with such commanders your goal may never be reached.

Ask yourself: What would be a great thing to do with my life before I die? Whatever it is, decide to do it! If it's more education you need, get it! If it's more money you need, find it! It's out there waiting to be invested in exciting new projects, plans, and people! If it's more talent you need, determine to acquire the skill—or hire the talent. Whatever you do—don't blow the opportunities that are still before you. God is desperately trying to instill a dream into your imagination. Don't torpedo it by saying it's impossible.

Your greatest danger will not be failure to reach your goal; the greatest danger is that you'll make it and stop growing. Understand that goal setting is a never-ending activity of living persons and institutions. It is the pulse beat that tells you there's life here. "I hope you live to see all your dreams come true, Dr. Schuller," someone said to me. I objected. "I hope I don't! Or I will have died before I die physically. When a man has reached his goals and fails to set new goals, he's stopped living and is merely existing. A man dies when he stops dreaming. Fear not that you shall die. Fear rather that you shall stop living before you die!"

This is a universal life principle: When an organism, an individual, or an institution stops growing, the seeds of decline, decay, and death are planted. Make your goals large enough or expandable enough so you will not be boxed in when you reach them. Otherwise you will start failing just when you have started succeeding. Remember the principle taught by A. N. Whitehead, the great English philosopher: "Most great dreams of great dreamers are not fulfilled: They're transcended." So get exciting goals and come alive!

3

PROBLEM-SOLVING PRINCIPLES THAT WORK

Now get set for problems. You can be assured that a project that doesn't run into problems isn't a worthwhile project. After you have established goals, you need only a well-developed Possibility Thinking attitude toward problems and you will succeed.

My friend Walter Burke, who became president of the MacDonnell Douglas Company during the early days of space exploration, said, "There is no such thing as an insolvable problem. What appears to be an impossible problem is merely a temporary roadblock to ingenuity." Under his dynamic leadership, the company was just completing the space lab scheduled for 1973 launching. He gave me a tour through this remarkable laboratory. Then we lunched together in his large, comfortable office. Behind his desk hung a huge specially framed copy of the *Possibility Thinkers Creed* which I had written some months before. (When he heard of it, he had asked for a copy.)

"It says everything we believe around here," he said. The creed is as follows:

> When faced with a mountain
> I will not quit.
> I will keep on striving
> until I
> climb over,
> find a pass through,
> tunnel underneath,
> or simply stay and
> turn the mountain
> into a gold mine!
> With God's help!

Then Walter Burke revealed this startling bit of information: "Years ago when I was studying aeronautical engineering, we were taught that no airplane could ever be built to break the sound barrier. First, it would have to be so large and overweight that it could never become airborne." He was smiling as he continued, "Furthermore our instructors taught us that if, by some remote possibility, future technology would make present impossible problems obsolete, enabling us to create an airplane that could actually fly faster than sound, it would still be impossible because any object that exceeded the speed of sound would break up into pieces." I need not tell my readers how false these beliefs were; if there were not people like Walter Burke who look for solutions and believe all things are possible, we would still be in the subsonic age.

"There's a solution to every problem," I had written in *Move Ahead with Possibility Thinking*. Not long after, I was talking on the telephone to a young girl in an eastern college who had read that line and was desperately calling to say she was facing a problem that defied solution. "Dr. Schuller," she said, her youthful voice cracking with tearful emotion, "I was going to be a chemistry major." She had just been called in to see the head of the department who told her that he had seen her name on the failing list in organic chemistry and wanted to know what was wrong? She wept hysterically at the other end of the line. When she recovered, she went on, "Dr. Schuller, you say there's a solution to every problem, but I don't see any solution to this problem! There are only three weeks left in the semester; if I fail this course, I'm finished!"

Being keenly aware of my lack of adequate wisdom on this subject, I was silently praying for guidance. When she finished, I heard myself say, "Look, go back and tell him that you must earn at least a B in this course. Tell him your whole career hinges on it. Tell him you are willing to do anything within your legal and moral code to earn a B. Ask him to think of any and every possible way in which you can succeed!"

She did exactly as she was advised. Her chemistry professor listened and was deeply moved at her dedication, sincerity, and strong-willed determination. "I'll tell you what I could do," he said, "I could give you an I for incomplete. During midsemester break you could hire a tutor and really study hard. Sometime during the first three weeks of the next semester, I'll give you two tests, which will include your final exam in this course. I'll average the two test grades and that will be your grade for the course."

She wept with new hope and joy as she ran across the campus to her room, dashed up two flights of stairs, threw her books on the bed, and rushed to the telephone to call me and share the good news. "There's hope," she cried. So she hired a tutor midterm. She concentrated, she asked questions, she worked problems day after day, until after spending six solid days in concentrated cramming, it all came together in her mind. She began solving problems that she was positive (three weeks earlier) she just did not have the brains to solve!

Two weeks into the second semester, she took the first of the two tests and received an A. A week later she took her final exam and pulled a B. Today her permanent academic record shows that she earned a B in organic chemistry.

The most important principle in a success-producing philosophy on problem solving can be summed up in six words: Never believe any problem is unsolvable. Even if you feel a problem is impossible do not surrender your planned goal to the domination of this negative feeling. Whatever you do, *never verbalize a negative emotion*. To verbalize a negative emotion will confuse your subconscious. You will give your doubts legs to stand on. You will support your fears and misgivings. Before you know it your dreams will be trampled under a herd of goal-squashing impossibility thoughts.

Beware of Negative Thinking Experts

I must warn you against the most dangerous and destructive force on earth. It is the *Negative Thinking Expert*. Because he is an expert you will be tempted to listen uncritically, trust him, and quit! Struck by the authoritative position that he holds, you will tend to believe him without question. We hear through our peer, not through our ear!

A Negative Thinking Expert is someone who is so well-informed, trained, and experienced on the subject that if it's never been successfully done before, he'll know it, and will not hesitate a moment to tell you. He will then, with the authoritative hauteur of a brilliant intellectual snob, enumerate all of the real or imaginary reasons why it never succeeded, convincing himself first, then you, that all of his words are proof positive that the whole idea is unrealistic, beyond credibility, ridiculous, unthinkable, and impossible. Thus he blocks progress, obstructs development, stifles creativity, halts advance thinking, and delays for months, years, or decades, the big breakthroughs.

Look For and Latch Onto Possibility Thinking Experts

A Possibility Thinking expert is a person who, when faced with a new concept, and knowing that it has never been done successfully before, is charged with excitement at what he sees as a great opportunity to become a pace-setting pioneer. He is stimulated by the opportunity to discover new solutions to old problems using the knowledge of a new age to make an historic breakthrough. Because he is convinced that there must be a way to overcome seemingly insurmountable difficulties, his creative powers are stimulated to produce amazing results. Using advanced research techniques, he proves that some long-accepted causes for past failure were, in fact, errors of judgment made by intelligent researchers who lacked the tools, skills, or related knowledge available in this modern age.

The Possibility Thinking expert often discovers that stated causes for such failures are really not causes but symptoms that blocked creative thinkers from further trying. As a resourceful researcher, the Possibility Thinker discovers the true causes and then by tapping the information bank of recent successful experimentation in related or even nonrelated fields, he constructs an innovative solution to a previously insolvable problem.

One spring evening the telephone rang in my home. "Are you the Dr. Schuller who wrote *Move Ahead with Possibility Thinking?*" a youthful voice asked. I admitted I was.

"I've got to see you," she said. "I want to find out if you're a phony or not."

Amazed at such direct frankness and realizing that my integrity was being challenged, I told her, "OK—be in my office tomorrow morning. Just drop in and I'll see you between appointments."

The next morning my secretary whispered over the intercom, "There's a young lady here, Miss Barbara Bassinger, who wants to see you. She said she spoke to you last night and you told her to come in."

"That's right. Send her in."

The door opened to the amazing sight of the strangest contraption I'd ever seen. Sitting in a wheelchair was a young girl surrounded by an incredible assemblage of metal and leather. A network of steel and leather straps started at her feet, crisscrossed at her ankles, and were connected to braces hinged at her knees. These were joined to metal straps along both of her thighs, which were bolted to an abdominal metal body belt. Two black shining eyes peered at me out of a mask also made of leather and steel. She raised a hand, and I saw that metal braces supported both of her arms.

"Surprised?" she said with a laughing voice.

"I must admit I've never seen anything like it before," I answered.

"I'm a cerebral palsied quadraplegic," she explained. "When I was a child the experts told my parents that I would never walk and I'd never be able to get very far in school. I grew up believing that also, until I heard the words, 'If you have faith as a grain of mustard seed, you will say to your mountain "move," and nothing will be impossible to you.' I found a doctor who was a Positive Thinking expert and asked him, 'Can't you devise something that will help me to walk?' Before he could answer I told him, 'If you put an iron brace between my ankles, then my legs won't fly around. And if you stretch my head with a neck brace, and hold it steady with iron bars bolted to a chest plate, and if you put iron braces between my arms to keep them from flying around . . .' He listened to me, and this is what he came up with. I thought you'd like to see it."

I was stunned. I felt pity flow through me toward her until she started talking again, "Now, Dr. Schuller, here is the good news. I CAN WALK!" And with a creak of leather and the clatter of iron, she rose from her wheelchair and walked around the room. Then she dropped back into her chair and proudly announced, "And I just got my MA degree from San Diego State College."

Look around you and you'll find someone you know, or have heard of, who is a great Possibility Thinker. Latch on to that person or his inspiring story when you are up against what might seem to be insufferable odds.

How to Develop a Success-Assuring Philosophy about Problem Solving

1. *Look for Problems:* Be the first to spot problems and you'll become the leader. Leadership goes to those who think ahead. The leader spots problems that lie years ahead, long before others suspect there could ever be future problems. He prepares a careful analysis of every possible problem together with a detailed list of solutions and well-thought-out recommendations as to alternatives.

A Possibility Thinker does not ignore problems when he is enthusiastically presenting his ideas. He knows there are some flaws in every idea. He keeps asking, "What's wrong with an idea?" not with the attitude of wanting to torpedo it, but with an attitude that will insure the life of the idea. By carefully thinking out answers to possible objections that might be raised, he meets problems before they arise. Thorough problem spotting is a mark of responsible leadership. As a leader of a church, I constantly try to envision problems we will face in five, ten, and twenty years from now.

2. *Anticipate Problems:* If you are the head of an organization and your organization has no problems, you really have a problem. Not to have a problem can be a serious problem. More often than not, it indicates that you are not moving ahead, or are not moving fast enough, or are not thinking big enough. Growth is always marked by difficulties. "Woe to those who are at ease in Zion."

"We need big problems to hold our team of engineers together," Walter Burke says. "If we can't feed them big challenges they will join a more aggressive company that can."

An organization that fails to expand its goals to keep challenges before the staff will surely lose its high-energy, dynamic, enthusiastic, brilliant men who thrive on problem-busting situations. For this reason, every top executive knows that unless he keeps the company expanding and growing, it will begin to die. Great goals keep Big People together. Remember this rule: Growth-restricting, goal-blocking obstacles must be removed at any cost, or the seeds of decay and death become planted in the person, organization, company, committee, or institution. Death starts when problems near solution. Renewal comes when urgent new problems arise, begging for creative solution.

3. *Welcome Problems:* Regard every problem as an opportunity. Leon Shimkin, chairman of the large publishing house of Simon and Schuster says, "We have no problems in our organization, only opportunities."

A problem (opportunity) may be the push you needed to remodel, retool, reorganize, restructure, rearrange, or relocate. Persons, traditions, organizations, and institutions, firmly ingrained in their well-worn systematic ways, must usually come face to face with enormous problems before they think of changing. Every problem is an opportunity to see something.

How does a leader sell an idea? First, he calls attention to a problem either existing or forthcoming. Second, he dramatizes the problem. Third, he emotionalizes the problem. Fourth, he enlarges the problem, pointing out that the problem will not go away if ignored, but will only become more serious. Next, he offers all possible solutions saving the best alternative—his idea—for the last. Then, he points out that the solution will never be easier, or cheaper (that really gets results) than right now. Of course he times his exposure of the problem carefully. He knows that if he waits until the problem becomes more complex he will be able to sell a bigger idea. He also knows if he moves too fast he'll only sell a repair. If he waits a little longer he can sell a replacement. Be patient and you will sell a pair of pants instead of a patch. Every leader, every salesman, every chief executive knows that without a real problem, he'll never be able to move ahead.

4. *Never Let Problems Stop You from Making the Right Decision:* Goal setting, based on a clear commitment to a value system, leads to swift and assured decision making. You always make a decision based on what you know is the right thing to do. *You do not wait to decide until you*

see solutions to every problem or problems, rather than possibilities, will assume leadership over your life. Just because you can't see solutions to problems doesn't give you the right to make the wrong decision. And to fail to make the right decision is to decide to make a wrong decision.

Never confuse problem-solving issues with decision-making issues. As I stated earlier, in our nonprofit, service-oriented business called church work, we ask big questions in the decision-making phase: "Will it help people who are hurting?" "Will it be a great thing for God?" "Is anybody else doing anything about it?" These are the decision-making questions. We do not consider at this decision-making stage any questions that properly belong in the problem-solving stage. I refer to such problem-solving questions as "What will it cost? Where will we get the money?" "Who can we get to do the job?" "How will we find the time and energy?"

Discussion of these problem-solving questions are premature and out of order in an initial decision-making meeting. Decisions, after all, are never made on the basis of whether all the problems are solvable. Decisions are based on the dictates of conscience, commitment, principle, policy, and personal or corporate honor. If it is the right thing to do—decide to do it!

By clarifying the distinction between decision making and problem solving, you will spare what might be a wasteful drain of creative energy. Enormous energy is lost in indecision by those who cannot make up their minds because they are unable to imagine solutions to problems they expect to encounter. Thus, indecision is tiresome and fatiguing!

Spare the mental energy that would be diffused through prolonged and confusing debate. Make the right decision and release enormous creative power by focusing on innovative solutions to problems.

Doublecheck your so-called problem. It may, in reality, be indecision. Do not expect God to show you solutions to the tough problems until you show Him that you have the faith to make the right decisions.

5. *Analyze Your Problems Accurately:* If there is a danger of confusing decisions with problems, there is also a

PROBLEM-SOLVING PRINCIPLES THAT WORK 45

danger of confusing symptoms with problems. Even experts do this sometimes.

A minister of a Protestant church was complaining that he was losing his congregation. "What is your biggest problem?" I asked. "Lack of skilled staff," he answered. The following conversation took place:

DR. SCHULLER: Why don't you have a skilled staff?

THE MINISTER: We can't afford it. We have real money problems.

DR. SCHULLER: Why do you have money problems?

THE MINISTER: Costs are going up, and membership is going down.

DR. SCHULLER: How did your membership growth the past year compare to your membership goals?

THE MINISTER: We didn't have growth goals and we didn't grow.

The minister really had only two problems. One was lack of growth goals. The other, more basic, was lack of Possibility Thinking leadership. All the other so-called problems were symptoms. He was advised to set growth goals, be a decision maker, and move ahead and solve his growth restricting problems.

That church is coming alive today. After analyzing over two thousand individual church situations in America, I have yet to find a single one that had a real money problem —it's always a lack-of-creative-ideas problem.

> Make a Decision and
> You Solve Your
> Problem

6. *Organize to Divide and Conquer Your Problem*: I stood in the "second story" of the MacDonnell-Douglas space lab and marveled at the incredibly efficient use of space. My guide explained the unbelievable number of "unsolvable" problems that were handled in this first three-man scientific laboratory to be sent into outer space.

"How did you solve so many complex problems?" I asked Mr. Burke. His answer contains universal principles that you can use: "No matter how big the problem is, break it down until you get the smallest lump, and solve it and then another—until you put the solved parts together like tinkertoys or pieces of a puzzle."

7. *Hire or Ask Smarter People Than You to Help:* If you are having trouble with your problem get others to help you. Remember: The bigger the challenge, the tougher the problem, and the greater is your chance to attract the support of outstanding Possibility Thinking experts.

If your problem is a common one it will be easy to find solutions. Others have. If, on the other hand, your problem is really unique, the first of its kind, or the biggest in its field, you may attract some of the smartest men in the world to assist.

"Success," according to Walter Burke, "is a matter of not quitting and failure is a matter of giving up too soon." With this philosophy of problem solving as a base, let's focus on four major problems you must solve to become the person you want to be.

4

SELF-CONFIDENCE—
GET IT! USE IT! KEEP IT!

A Dutch immigrant boy longs to become a major league ballplayer. He imagines himself standing on the pitcher's mound. At the age of nineteen he is there—on the threshold of his dream.

A twenty-year-old Mexican woman, the mother of two children who have been abandoned by her husband, finds herself in a strange city called Los Angeles. She speaks only Spanish and her worldly wealth consists of the seven dollars in her pocketbook. She determines to take care of her children and make a new life for herself. She believes she can do it—and she does!

What do these two persons have in common? A positive self-image. A miracle-working force called self-confidence. They have it and everybody needs it. If you don't have it, you can get it. It will help unlock the door to an amazing future.

A lack of self-confidence is one of the four most common failure-producing factors that must be overcome if you hope to become the person you want to be. Believe me, mountains melt before the self-reliant, self-confident person.

Henry Ford said, "Think you can, think you can't; either way you'll be right." Be careful of what you imagine yourself becoming. There is an abundance of scientific evidence that an individual's mental picture of himself, more than any other factor, sets the ultimate boundaries of his achievements. We now know that the human brain, like an intricate automatic guidance system, will steer your life toward a realization of the mental self-image you feed into it. Your subconscious will work for you or against you. You make the determination by the self-fulfilling dreams or the self-defeating limitations you feed into it. When this law is understood and applied, we see revolutionary changes in human personality. Deeply ingrained habits, fundamental behavior patterns, even talents and abilities, have been miraculously altered by persons who have believed, acted upon, and used this law of self-image psychology.

"What do you want to be when you grow up?" I asked thirteen-year-old Bert Blyleven.

"A baseball player," the kid from Holland answered crisply. Not too many years before he had emigrated to American from the Netherlands along with his parents and six brothers and sisters. Soon they were filling a pew in my church every Sunday.

"That's a great big wonderful dream, Bert," I said. "Believe it and you will succeed." Five years later he graduated from high school. "What are you going to do now, Bert?" I asked.

"Play baseball!" he answered confidently.

Before that summer was over he was playing in a minor league team in the Midwest. With the coming of winter Bill Rigney, manager of the Minnesota Twins, was scouting the "young kids" of the minor leagues in their Florida training ground.

"That Bert Blyleven has something!" he said to a close friend. The following summer Bert was rolling up an impressive record in the minor leagues when he received a long-distance call.

"Bert Blyleven, this is Bill Rigney speaking. I want you to get on the next plane to Washington, D.C. I want to see you." That ended the cryptic call.

What did Rigney want? Certainly he couldn't be planning to take a recent high school graduate with barely a year's experience in minor league play and put him in the major leagues?

The Washington monument loomed against the skyline as the jet approached the airport. The teenage Dutch kid was big-eyed as he walked off the plane in the Capitol city of his adopted country.

"Hi Bert! Welcome to Washington!" It was Bill Rigney.

"What do you want me for?" the aspiring youngster asked.

"Bert," Rigney said looking him straight in the eye, "I've got a problem." He paused, then continued, "Louis Tiant

SELF-CONFIDENCE—GET IT! USE IT! KEEP IT! 49

has a bad shoulder and I need a pitcher badly. I've watched you carefully."

Bert's heart was pounding. "Bert!" the manager of the Minnesota Twins squared off and let him have it, "I've decided to start you on the mound tomorrow night when we face Washington. Do you think you can handle it?"

"Yes sir! I'll try," the youthful voice was ripe with confidence.

"I hope Bill Rigney knows what he's doing! That boy is only nineteen. He's got to be the youngest kid playing in the majors," a Minnesota fan observed. Under the brilliant lights of the huge ballpark the boyish freckle-faced Hollander warmed up. Suddenly the strains of the national anthem filled the air as the Stars and Stripes were unfurled. The crowd sang the lines with patriotic fervor. Bert's lips moved—but no sounds came out. Then came the great announcement, "Play ball." Bert Blyleven's dream was about to come true.

This was the moment he had dreamed about all his life. Thousands of eyes were riveted on him. Radio announcers were sharing the exciting moment with the anxious fans listening in Minnesota. Bert threw his first ball.

"Strike!" the umpire called. "Ball." "Strike." "Ball." "Ball."

With a 3 to 2 count, the greenhorn pitcher settled down, peered for a sign from the catcher, raised his arms clutching the ball, and shot it like a bullet to the plate. A crack like the sound of a rifle snapped through the stadium as the veteran batter, a heavyweight in the Washington lineup, connected with the crucial pitch.

Young Bert spun around on the pitcher's mound to see the white ball rise high, soaring up, on, and over like a jet plane until it cleared the fence for a clean home run.

It could have devastated him. Instead, a small voice deep within him whispered, "O.K. Bert—you can do it. You've got what it takes—show them. If you don't they'll tag you as a loser. Here's your chance to really prove your stuff." Calmly he faced the next batter.

"Strike-out," the umpire called as the number two man in the lineup fell for a brilliant curve ball. "Strike-out!" Bert was to hear that happy sound again and again, as for seven innings he stunned the crowd with a brilliant debut! He was on his way to an impressive career.

Imagineering Your Way to Success

This process of mentally picturing yourself as succeeding has been called "imagineering." I keep seeing the astounding achievements of those who engineer solutions to production problems by imagining that they can succeed.

As commencement exercises were drawing to a close in Azusa Pacific College, Azusa, California, the most honored and brilliant students were receiving their Bachelor of Arts degrees. In that small select group of outstanding students, there were three who stood out. One was a black man, one was an Indian, and one was a sightless girl who carried a white cane. The black man, the Indian, the blind girl—all three were graduating magna cum laude. All three had been listed in *Who's Who in American Colleges and Universities*. I am sure that all three might have easily become miserable failures. They might have developed a negative, cynical attitude, blaming their failures on their disadvantaged childhood or a prejudiced society. However, these three made it to the top. Why? How? What made the difference?

I spoke to the sightless girl afterward and asked, "What's your secret?" With beaming face, the tassel swaying over the edge of her mortarboard, she unfurled her faith. "My secret is in a Bible verse I learned years ago." She quoted the power-packed sentence, "I can do all things through Christ who strengthens me."

Some people make victims of their disadvantages, while other people are victimized by their disadvantages. The black man, the Indian, and the sightless girl had one thing in common. They believed in the power of Jesus Christ to change their lives, and their situations. When you believe in Jesus Christ, you begin to believe that with him you can overcome. And you can reach the top'

Four Dynamic Qualities Mark the Self-Confident Winner

Imagination: The self-confident person imagines himself

SELF-CONFIDENCE—GET IT! USE IT! KEEP IT!

being the person he wants to become. He ignores the way he is now.

Commitment: So strong is the desire to achieve his dream that the self-confident person totally commits himself to his goal. It is an unconditional, nonnegotiable commitment. The power of a totally committed person is incalculable.

Affirmation: First imagine. Then commit. Now affirm that you are going to succeed. Verbalize your positive thinking. This will exercise and vitalize your self-confidence. At the same time, you will cause others to believe in your eventual success. Now a wonderful thing happens. As other people begin to believe in you they will want to help, which adds fresh propellant to your rocketing self-confidence!

Never Give Up: Never, Never, Never, give up! Patience and persistence are the crowning qualities of self-confident champions. Defeat and failure are heretical concepts that cannot and will not be contemplated.

The initials of these four qualities spell I C-A-N! That's self-confidence! Properly directed and constructively channeled, self-confidence becomes the very power of Almighty God surging, throbbing, pulsating, vibrating with the force of spiritual electricity through the human personality, transforming a listless, lifeless, apathetic person into an inspired, inflamed dynamo who catapults his life to greatness!

"I Can"—*The Two Most Powerful Words in Your Vocabulary*

"I can," said Cyrus W. Field when the project of laying the first Atlantic cable was called a wild fantastic undertaking.

"I can," said Tracy Barnes when wiser people knew you couldn't make a transcontinental balloon flight across the U.S. After three thousand miles and five months in the air, he did it—all the way from San Diego, California, to Villas, New Jersey. Floating on capricious and unpredictable air movements, he had met exciting and dangerous experiences. He crashed into a mountain peak one hundred miles east of San Diego and spent three days in a hospital with a sprained back. He got lost in the Rockies and was separated from his ground crew for three days. Several times the balloon snagged on trees forcing delays. He landed near Pittsburgh.

It wasn't all rough going for the twenty-seven-year-old balloonist. He purposely drifted to the bottom of the Grand Canyon, parked his wicker basket and balloon, and went swimming in the Colorado River. From Nebraska to Pittsburgh it was a breeze. "Just great," Barnes said. The trip took about twice as long as estimated because of the unfavorable winds and the many mishaps.

"I can," said Birt Duncan. As a cast-off Negro child in the South, he was bumped from foster home to foster home. He remembers living with more than thirteen families from Arkansas to Mississippi. Often he'd fall asleep in classrooms because of improper nourishment. However, he now has a PhD from Princeton in psychology and is completing work for an MD degree at the University of California in San Diego.

"What's really important is not what color your skin is—white or black," Birt Duncan says, "more important is—what color is your thinking? Red? Or Green? Think Green. Think Go! You cannot control the color of your skin, but you can determine the color of your thinking!"

"I can," said Romana Bañuelos. She was only sixteen years old when she married in Mexico. Two years and two sons later, she was divorced and working for one dollar a day in an El Paso laundry.

She heard she could do better in California, so with seven dollars in her pocket she took a bus to Los Angeles.

Starting by washing dishes and then taking whatever job she could get, she saved as much money as she could. When she had four hundred dollars, she and an aunt bought a little tortilla factory that had one tortilla machine and a grinder in a showcase in the front. When the aunt wanted to leave the business, Romana bought her share.

Romana's Mexican Food Products became the largest Mexican wholesale food concern in the nation, grossing five million dollars a year and Romana employs over three hundred people.

Romana was determined to lift the level of Mexican-Americans. "We need our own bank," she thought. She helped found the Pan-American National Bank in East Los

Angeles to serve the Mexican-American community. The bank's resources are more than twenty-two million dollars with 86 percent of the depository of Latin ancestry.

"I can," Romana said when Negative Thinking Experts told her "Mexican-Americans can't start a bank," "You're not qualified," "You can't make it." Undaunted, she spearheaded a committee which hired three attorneys who obtained a charter for the new bank.

"We opened the bank in a little trailer," she says, "but selling stock to the community was a problem. The people didn't have any faith in themselves. I used to go and ask them if they would buy stock and they said, 'Oh, Mrs. Bañuelos, what makes you think we can have a bank? We've tried for ten or fifteen years and always failed. You see, Mexican people are not bankers.'" The bank is now one of East Los Angeles' dynamic success stories!

"What's the major problem that keeps the Mexican-Americans down today?" she was asked. Her answer: "They believe the lie they have been told about themselves —that Mexicans are inferior! I was raised as a child in Mexico and no one can make me believe that lie! I'm proud of my Mexican ancestry!"

Today Romana Bañuelos has reached new heights of success. She was handpicked by the President of the United States to be the thirty-fourth treasurer of the United States!

Expect More of Yourself

Not only Mexican-Americans but many other people rise no higher than their expectation level. If you expect little or nothing from yourself, don't be surprised if you amount to nothing.

Perhaps you have an inferiority complex because proud or prejudiced society has been telling you a lie about yourself. Perhaps you did poorly in school and have concluded you're not very bright. Don't believe it! You may have had a poor teacher.

In a recent *Reader's Digest* article Harvard psychologist Robert Rosenthal wondered, "Do some children perform poorly in school because their teachers expect them to?" If so, Rosenthal surmised, then raising the teacher's expectations should raise the children's performance. He was ready to try his theory in actual classrooms. Kindergarten through fifth-grade pupils in a cooperating school were given a new test of learning ability. The following September, after the tests were graded, the teachers were casually given the names of five or six children in each new class who were designated as "spurters" possessing exceptional learning ability.

What the teachers didn't know was that the names had been picked in advance of the tests on a completely random basis. The difference between the chosen few and the other children existed only in the minds of the teachers.

The same tests taken at the end of the school years revealed that the spurters had actually soared far ahead of the other children, gaining as many as 15 to 27 IQ points. Their teachers described them as happier than the other children, more curious, more affectionate, and having a better chance of being successful in later life. Obviously, the only change had been one of attitudes. Because the teachers had been led to expect more of certain students, those children came to expect more of themselves.

"The explanation probably lies in the subtle interaction between teacher and pupils," says Rosenthal. "Tone of voice, facial expressions, touch and posture may be the means by which—often unwittingly—she communicated her expectations to her pupils. Such communication may help a child by changing his perceptions of himself."

Dr. Floyd Baker, a member of the Garden Grove Community Church, is a professor of physics. He recently wrote a special paper for his doctorate in physics. In it is an illuminating confession:

> I first entered the teaching profession in 1960 and brought with me a set of attitudes toward instruction and student-teacher interaction. Now in retrospect, I had what I know today to be a bad attitude toward my students and their motivation. I recall I used to say to them at the beginning of the semester, "You have to pass this course or you might as well change your major. I am the ONLY one teaching this class, so you might as well get along as best you can. I don't like people who won't study, so get on the ball! I give you the material and all you have to do is learn it. Let me tell you, about 50 percent of you won't pass. Don't let it be YOU!" As you can see, I always gave the students superb confidence. Well, amazingly, my predictions always came true . . . 50 percent flunked out . . . always, year after year. I would

get together with the other college professors and we would drink coffee and we would laugh at the number of dropouts that we had in our classes. We used to say that the one who received the most dropouts was the most successful teacher. I know now that this is a bad attitude. About this time, my wife and I started attending a very dynamic church. The ministers were all enthusiastic and all preached outstanding sermons. Each week, when I attended church, I was deluged with the need for positive thinking and enthusiasm in everything you do. I discovered that you are always received better if you have a positive attitude when visiting or talking to people. However, my problems were, how can I inspire and enthuse my students?

The ministers kept saying, "If you have a problem, through prayer and reading the Bible, you can find the answer." I started reading my Bible, chapter after chapter, book after book. I came to First Corinthians 13 and I found the key. From then on, Christ was in my life, I went in front of my class and I said to them, "I want every one of you to pass. And it is my job to see that you do. The material is difficult, but if we work together, every student in this class can pass and learn a great deal." There was a different atmosphere in the classes from then on and I thank God and Christ for this spirit. The dropout and failure rate prior to Christ being in my classroom was 50 percent. However, when I applied this new positive technique, with the cooperation of the students, *every student passed!* One received a C plus, one a B minus, and the rest all got Bs and As and I NEVER CHANGED MY GRADING PROCEDURE ONE BIT!!

Remember: Goethe said, "Treat people as if they were what they ought to be and you help them to become what they are capable of being."

God Believes in You—He Can't Be Wrong!

The beggar sat across the street from an artist's studio. From his window the portrait painter sketched the face of the defeated, despairing soul—with one important change. Into the dull eyes he put the flashing glint of an inspired dreamer. He stretched the skin on the man's face to give him a look of iron will and fierce determination. When the painting was finished, he called the poor man in to see it. The beggar did not recognize himself. "Who is it?" he asked as the artist smiled quietly. Then, suspecting that he saw something of himself in this portrait, he hesitantly questioned, "Is it me? *Can* it be me?" "That's how I see you," replied the artist. Straightening his shoulders, the beggar responded, "If that's the man you see—that's the man I'll be."

God looks at you and sees a beautiful person waiting to be born! If you could see in a vision the man God meant you to be, never again could you be quiet. You'd rise up and try and succeed.

They tell us that ants are born with wings and use them, know the glory and flame and rapture of flight, then tear these wings off deliberately, choosing to live their lives out as crawling insects. Choosing that when God gave them the vast empire of the air! Don't make the same mistake by selling yourself short!

You Can Do It!

So you have never amounted to anything? You're a nobody? You're imprisoned in a mental dungeon of self-condemnation, self-flagellation? Break loose! It's as easy as A, B, C.

A—Affirm: "Others can do it—others *are doing it*. So can I!

B—Believe: "God has a better life in store for me!"

C—Choose: "Break loose from the hypnotizing forces of negative thoughts that imprison me."

The Bastille had become a symbol of total tyranny. "It's impossible to break out," everyone said. So everyone believed it. One day the poor imprisoned souls were driven beyond endurance. Like madmen they stormed the place in what seemed a hopeless attack. To their astonishment they found it garrisoned by only thirty troopers. In only four hours it fell! The impossible was done! The Bastille was down!

For years you have believed you could never break loose and succeed. Well you can! It's as simple as A-B-C.

Self-confidence—Here's How to Get It

1. Psychiatrists may help you. If your self-image is so negative that you find yourself entertaining suicidal thoughts, you should seek professional help. Depth analysis may help uncover some ego-damaging experiences in early child-

SELF-CONFIDENCE—GET IT! USE IT! KEEP IT!

hood. By all means seek out a psychiatrist who believes in belief! In New York City there is a religious-psychiatric clinic connected with the Marble Collegiate Church. A branch of that clinic operates on the West Coast in the Tower of Hope, on the campus of our Garden Grove Community Church.

2. "Props" can be self-confidence boosters. Where some people will need serious professional help in their pursuit of self-confidence, others may need only the help of simple props. In *The Devil's Advocate,* Morris West tells of one character who simply put a fresh carnation in the lapel of his coat and faced the world with confidence! A hair style will do the same for others. A new set of sharp clothes may do the trick for you. Perhaps you need to trim off a few pounds before you begin to feel self-confident. Plastic surgery, Maxwell Maltz reported, transformed many a patient from a self-degrading to a self-complimenting person!

But remember! These are material props. They may give your self-confidence a needed boost; however, a lasting self-confidence must have deeper spiritual roots to survive the fall and winter seasons of the soul's journey through life.

3. People who inspire you can do wonders in giving birth and bolstering power to self-confidence. Seek out the friendship of and surround yourself with people who build your self-esteem.

A world famous opera star was slated to give a concert in the Paris Opera House, which was packed with eager fans. Just before the performance, the manager stepped in front of the curtain and announced, "We regret to inform you that the star you hoped to hear tonight is suffering from laryngitis and will not be able to perform." A gasp of disappointment rose from the audience. "However," he continued, "I'm pleased to introduce a new performer of great promise who will sing for you this evening." The unknown singer sang his first selection with excellence. When he finished he was received with icy stillness by the disappointed audience. Nobody applauded! The darkened auditorium was cold and insultingly quiet. Suddenly from an upper balcony came an enthusiastic child's voice, "Daddy, I think you were wonderful." Then it happened. Applause suddenly broke out, loud and long!

President Theodore Roosevelt was proud of his first three sons when they announced their intention to join the military service. But when his fourth son also decided to go into uniform, the tough Rough-Rider resisted. "Not all my boys," he argued. To which his wife replied, "Ted, if you raise them as eagles you can't expect them to fly like sparrows."

The author and playwright William Saroyan was inspired to self-confidence at the age of thirteen. He had just purchased a typewriter. His esteemed granduncle Garabed visited him not too long after.

"My boy, what's that contraption?" the old gent asked.

"A typewriter, sir," the lad answered.

"What's it for?"

"For clear writing, sir." And William handed him a sample.

"What's this writing?"

"Philosophical sayings."

"Whose?"

"Mine, sir."

The wise old fellow studied the sheet and then handed it back to his nephew and said, "Proceed, for it is not impossible to walk on water."

"I knew then I could do it," William Saroyan recalls. Self-confidence, strong enough to last him a lifetime, was born within him then and there!

4. Pluck, that resourceful spirit that motivates an individual to risk failure in trying to do something on his own really builds self-confidence. Self-confidence cannot be bought, or taught; it must be caught! You catch it when you take a chance, and make it!

> Pluck Is Trying Harder
> Than You Ever Have
> Before

One mile from my office in the Garden Grove Community Church in California is Disneyland—a fabulous success story. Few people ever demonstrated more self-reliance than its founder, Walt Disney. How did he get it?

"When I was nearly twenty-one years old I went broke for the first time," Disney recalled before his death. "I slept on cushions from an old sofa and ate cold beans out of a can. Then I set out for Hollywood." Reflecting on his subsequent success, the Grand Man of Movieland uttered this priceless statement, "I didn't know what I couldn't do so I was willing to take a chance and try anything."

Walt Disney liked to tell the story of the boy who wanted so much to march in the circus parade. When the show came to town the bandmaster needed a trombonist, so the boy signed up. He hadn't marched a block when his horrible sounds created pandemonium. "Why didn't you tell me you couldn't play a trombone?" the bandmaster demanded. The boy answered simply, "How did I know? I never tried before!"

Try Something Small

It's like learning to walk. The child takes first one faltering step, then the next. And so you also build belief in yourself by starting small and, as you succeed, taking larger steps.

I understand that the suspension bridge over Niagara was built in this fashion. First a kite was flown across the foaming falls. Attached to the kite was a thread, attached to the thread was a rope, attached to the rope was a cable. And so the cables and the other pieces were moved together until a great bridge spanned the chasm!

Start small—and succeed. Succeed where you are—then move on to bigger things. "Lift where you stand," Edward Barrett wisely said. As Booker T. Washington put it, "Cast down your buckets where you are."

God's Plan for Your Life

Finding and following God's plan for your life is the soundest, surest way to self-confidence. Already God is revealing to you His plan for your life. He is stimulating your imagination as you read this book. He has started to work in your life. Be sure God finishes what He starts! "For it is

God at work in you giving you the will and the power to achieve His purpose." (Phil. 2:13.)

"Be confident in this one thing—that God who has begun a good work in you shall complete it." (Phil. 1:6.)

Lawrence Welk published his autobiography *Wunnerful, Wunnerful* a few years ago. His inspiring success story reminds me of the Bible verse, "The eagle stirreth up her nest that the young might learn to fly."

God often allows problems to shake us up in order to get us out of a rut and onto the beautiful road He has planned for us. Lawrence might have spent his life as a farmer in North Dakota—except for a "terrible" thing that happened. He was a small boy on the edge of his teenage years when he awoke one morning deathly ill. At the nearest hospital, seventy-five miles away, it was found he had a ruptured appendix. Peritonitis had already set in, poison ravaged his body. A tube was inserted in his side to siphon off the deadly pollution. Feverish days turned into frightening weeks. Miraculously he survived. Through the long months of recuperation in the family's farmhouse he began to play sounds on his father's old accordion.

He began to believe in a divine plan for his life. "It seemed to me that God had given me a second chance at life and I prayed for guidance to use my life in ways that would please Him most."

The rest of the story is history. He visualized what he wanted. He actualized. He went to work on it. He realized his dreams. So can you.

Paint a mental picture of the *new you!* You are going to change. You are changing now. You will become the person you always wanted to be. Believe this.

Now discard all old mental pictures of yourself. These negative portraits are past history. Replace them with the future dream portrait of the person you want to become.

Computer programmers have an expression called "Gigo," which stands for Garbage In-Garbage Out. Feed garbage into the computer and garbage will come out. If you are failing, the problem is "Fifo"—failure pictures have been fed into your mind so failure comes out. Now, try the "Siso" formula! Success In-Success Out! Feed success pictures into your imagination and success *will* come out!

It's happening all around you today. Disadvantaged, defected, discouraged people are learning how to change their lives, their futures, their destinies. Now it's your turn to stop failing and start succeeding. Discover the better idea God has for your life. You are God's idea and God only dreams up beautiful ideas. He's expecting great things from you. Cooperate! Believe in yourself, NOW, and draw the possibilities out of your being.

5

PLAY THE POSSIBILITY THINKING GAME—AND WIN!

Let's check your progress so far:
1. You have begun to firm up goals in your mind.
2. You have developed a positive attitude in handling problems when they arise.
3. You have developed self-confidence—you know you can do it!

You are now ready to be entrusted with the most valuable secret I have to share with you. It will give you the key to creativity, solving your second biggest problem: How to become a truly creative person. Without the development of the art of creative thinking your dreams will quickly be grounded.

If you can become a creative, inventive way-finder, you will truly turn your dreams into exciting reality!

Is creativity a gift or is it an art? Is it an inherited talent that you have—or don't have? Or is it a skillful way of thinking that can be artfully learned by any person? There is abundant and mounting evidence that the latter is the truth.

Dr. Edwin H. Land, inventor of the Polaroid camera, has experimented with this phenomenon of creativity. He has placed blue collar workers alongside practicing, creative people, active in research. "It's amazing—the blue collar people are all becoming creative," he reports!

Among those trillions of cells in your brain, there lie thousands of brilliant but slumbering cells that are charged with vast powers waiting to be aroused, harnessed, and unleashed. If you can discover a way to stimulate them, you'll be amazed at your own brilliance and intelligence.

There is a clever technique that anyone can learn and use to stimulate these dormant cells. You'll become an amazing creative thinker, astonishing those who thought they knew you so well, with a stunning new skillful ability to create, invent, and innovate!

I call this technique *Playing the Possibility Thinking Game*. You can learn to play this game! It's free! It's fun! It's fruitful! It's simple! It's challenging! It's exciting! It's rewarding! I promise that it will revolutionize your future.

Don't let the word "game" fool you. Impregnated in the word are enormous creativity-releasing forces. We know that creativity takes place when a mind is deeply relaxed. A problem solver may wrestle unsuccessfully with his problem for long hours and finally retire. In the darkness of the early morning hours, he awakens with the bright idea.

It was so with Paul Fisher, who invented the remarkable pen with which I'm writing this book. He saw the need for a ball-point pen that could write on the ceiling, upside down, over grease, and underwater. It had never been done. All ball-points worked on the gravity principle. He spent a million dollars and months of time trying to make a breakthrough. At three o'clock one morning he awoke with the secret that made the invention possible. The Fisher pen was taken to the moon. It met NASA's requirement for a leakproof, longer-life-span, gravity-free-flowing instrument for writing in outer space.

Deep relaxation allows subconscious creativity-blocking tension to be removed, permitting the clever concept to flow with gleaming light into the conscious mind. The late Richard Neutra, the architect who is remembered as one of the most creative men of the century, did his best work from four until seven every morning. His subconscious was deeply relaxed at that hour of the day.

As I write these words I am on a cruise ship in the South Pacific. Tranquil seas, free-floating clouds, and the relaxing sounds of the water and the ship sweep away the tension and pressure of responsibility. Creative ideas flow fast and free.

Sitting in the gentle sunlight on a deckchair, I am surrounded by people. I realize I will not be bothered with meaningful interruptions. A passenger may stop to chat. This creates no tension because the interruption concerns no responsibilities. In my usual habitat, I found creative ideas flowed to me when I was sheltered from the possibility of unwelcome, responsibility-laden interruptions.

Anticipating pressure-laden interruptions produces enough tension on a deep level to block creativity. At home I find my brightest ideas flowing either when I'm alone in my car or when I'm flying in an airplane. At these times I cannot be reached by telephone, telegraph, a secretary's buzzer, or a knock on the door. This may explain why many people get their best ideas sitting in a church service! It also reveals a reason why the very early morning hours are so fruitful. Then, defensive tensions generated by the expectation of interruptions are not present. You know that nobody will bother you at five in the morning. So you are deeply relaxed. You are also free from the tensions that collect as the day unfolds. The vital telephone call, the letter, or a caller bring problems and produce tension-generating pressures. By the end of the usual day, you're like my cruise ship. She has been late arriving at several ports o' call. Why? She has been at sea for one year without having the bottom cleaned. Barnacles have collected slowly, steadily reproducing until the layers of encrustation are thick enough to slow the ship's speed by two knots an hour. So the swift flow of early morning creative thinking is slowly encrusted with the weight of tension-collecting experiences as noontime approaches. Some bad news, an upset, a rejection, a setback—the tension mounts by midday as you anticipate more difficulties.

Creativity is related to deep relaxation. The very word "work" generates pressure-producing tension. Work means responsibility. This implies accountability, which in turn produces subconscious creativity-blocking tension. The word "game" suggests freedom from responsibility and accountability; it implies a spirit of sportsmanship, which implies exciting race running, and risk taking (within boundaries that are quite safe). Because it is only a game, your subconscious mind will relax knowing you are free from vulnerability!

Consider the mind-set that results from the "game attitude":

1. *Risk-running:* The *fear* of failure is absent! If I lose —it's only a game." You *dare* to think in almost reckless dimensions. This is the arena where progress is always made.

2. *Record-breaking:* This mental attitude causes you to think bigger, reach farther, try harder, than you ever have before. You are putting yourself in a frame of mind where you've solved one of your greatest creativity-blocking problems, namely, how to *think bigger than you have ever thought before.* Almost always the inventive solution to every problem is that simple. Spend more money. Hire more people. Form a new organization. Travel farther. Telephone that expert in Europe, etc.

3. *Freedom-from-Commitment:* Since it's only a game, you can quit anytime you want and not ruin your reputation. You are free from the subconscious tension generated by the fear of involvement where you suspect you might get trapped by ongoing responsibilities. Because it's only a game, you can relax in total freedom from responsibility.

Generate a Mental Climate Conducive to Creativity

The word "possibility" is another key to success of this formula. The very word creates a mental climate, conducive to creativity. Simply think that it might be possible and you will begin to release creative brain cells from their invisible prison of subconscious defense mechanisms. To understand the cybernetic power of this word, consider its antonym, that dirty ten-letter-word "impossible." When uttered aloud, this word is devastating in its effect. Thinking stops. Progress is halted. Doors slam shut. Research comes to a screeching halt. Further experimentation is torpedoed. Projects are abandoned. Dreams are discarded. The brightest and the best of the creative brain cells nose-dive, clam up, hide out, cool down, and turn off in some dark but safe subterranean corner of the mind. By this defensive maneuver, the brain shelters itself against the painful sting of insulting disappointments, brutal rejections, and dashed hopes.

Let someone utter the magic words "It's possible." Those stirring words, with the siren appeal of a marshaling trumpet, penetrate into the subconscious tributaries of the mind, challenging and calling those proud powers to turn on, and turn out! Buried dreams are resurrected. Sparks of fresh enthusiasm flicker, then burst into new flame. Tabled motions are brought back to the floor. Dusty files are reopened. Lights go on again in the long darkened laboratories. Telephones start ringing. Typewriters make clattering music. Budgets are revised and adopted. "Help Wanted" signs are hung out. Factories are retooled and reopened. New products appear. New markets open. The recession has ended. A great new era of adventure, experimentation, and expansion and prosperity is born.

Now—Play the Possibility Thinking Game—
Here's How

Begin by believing that you possess latent gifts of creativity. You will respect, trust, and admire your own thoughts. Every person can be creative.

The old El Cortez Hotel in San Diego, California, had a problem. It desperately needed a new elevator to service the new rooftop dining room. Expert engineers and architects were consulted. Plans were formulated. It could be done, they agreed, by cutting through and eliminating choice rooms on every floor, by building new shafts and excavating below the basement level. It was a costly and unsatisfactory solution.

As the experts were discussing the project, a hotel employee overheard the conversation. He was concerned about the dust and dirt that would swirl through every floor during the construction period. Ambling over to the smartly dressed authorities, he blurted out, "Why don't you build it on the outside of the building?" Nobody had thought of that! Today the glass cage rises on the exterior of the hotel, giving guests a spectacular view of the harbor as they ascend to the roof. It has been imitated and copied around the world, but it was the first of its kind!

Ready to play the game? You can play it alone. However, it is far more dynamic if you will get together with at least one other Possibility Thinking person to try to dream up all sorts of serious (and ridiculous) ways to make your impossible dream become a possible dream!

You agree that you'll let your imagination run wild. Your moral and ethical principles will be the only limitations on your imagination. Begin by writing the numbers one through ten down the side of a blank piece of paper. Challenge all participants to dream up ten ways to reach

PLAY THE POSSIBILITY THINKING GAME—AND WIN! 67

the particular goal or solve the problem or bring that impossible dream into the realm of probability. Remember—anything goes. The wilder the idea, the better.

Visiting a friend in Japan, I made the flippant comment, "I think a walk-in-drive-in church would go over great in Japan."

He looked puzzled.

"It would pass the four success-determining questions," I said seriously, and elaborated:

1. Is it a practical idea? Yes! It would be possible for many people to worship in their cars who would never go into a traditional church.

2. Is it a pacesetting idea? Yes! It's never been done before. You'd get thousands of dollars worth of publicity.

3. Is it an inspiring idea? Yes! It could be a place of visual and audio beauty!

4. Is it an excellent idea? Yes! It could excel all other religious developments in size and service!

By this time I was so enthused I jumped up and said, "Ted, let's do it!"

"Impossible Bob," he said, adding, "ten acres of land out here would cost five million dollars."

I was floored.

He went on, "And you and I know that it's not possible for a church to generate enough income to pay off such an enormous base cost."

"OK Ted—so we know it's impossible. Let's just pretend that it might be possible—somehow! Let's play the Possibility Thinking Game. Ready?"

We laughed. How could a church with no members possibly swing a five-million-dollar land purchase? We made a mental list of possible ways: Find one donor to contribute five million. Find five donors to give one million each. We verbalized these rather ridiculous and unrealistic possibilities and sure enough arrived at a third possible way: Get one million people around the world to donate five dollars each. Hire an advertising agency. Place honest, inspiring, emotion-packed ads to sell the Million Member Club idea to Christians in England, Germany, Holland, Canada, and America. A $250,000 well-planned and well-placed promotional package might succeed. Rent the mailing lists of people around the world who donate to mission causes. It could work. As we voiced this plan, we called to action the brightest brain cells. They came up with the fourth idea: Set up a Corporation of Christians. Let them buy ten acres. Use seven acres for parking. On three landscaped garden acres erect three thirty-story structures to house the branch offices of the most prestigious Japanese firms. Then erect a cultural center for the performing arts for use by the community for music and drama—reserving in the lease arrangment the use of the building for church purposes every Sunday morning. Select a strategic site on the expressway between Tokyo and Yokohama. It could work. It is really feasible.

The Possibility Thinking Game worked again! Try it yourself. Use it to tackle any problem—big or small. But follow these rules carefully:

1. *Agree to Listen:* With a possibility-tuned ear listen to those strange, wonderful, creative ideas that creep into the back corner of your mind. Dare to express them—all of them! No matter how crazy they may seem. You won't worry about being laughed at. After all, it's only a game, you remind yourself. Meanwhile this rule, which the players have agreed upon, demands that every player honestly listen to every idea offered. No idea is scorned, snubbed, sneered, or scoffed at as an impossible suggestion.

2. *Agree to Care:* The game of Possibility Thinking must have a basically serious objective. There must be some deep inner concern that gets the game started and keeps it going. If you're playing the game trying to dream up ten possible ways to make a million dollars when you don't really care to make a million dollars, your most creative brain cells won't be stirred into action. Only when the subconscious mind deeply believes the mind-bending project to be very, very important—then, and only then will the hidden powers slumbering deep in the dark regions of the unconscious rise up and awaken into creative consciousness. The Possibility Thinking Game will produce serious and exciting new ideas if the minds playing the game really, really care!

One day in a round-table discussion, Norman Shumway, the esteemed surgeon who pioneered heart transplants, was asked whether artificial hearts would ever be invented.

"Impossible," he said. And then he explained, "It would

PLAY THE POSSIBILITY THINKING GAME—AND WIN! 69

require an unfailing permanent power-generating source." To settle the argument, he declared, "and if we had that, you wouldn't need gas tanks in your car." With that comment all members of the panel were stopped cold. All further discussions focused on subjects such as how can we overcome the body-rejection of-foreign-tissue problems.

Some weeks later, I mentioned the problem of constructing an artificial heart to a couple of associates, and we decided to play the Possibility Thinking Game and tackle this impossibility. We challenged our imaginations to come up with ten ways to solve the problem. To us it was a game. Still, we cared deeply in the sense that we knew that the invention of an artificial heart would be a priceless advance in human welfare, if it were possible. I don't recall all of the "way-out" ideas we listed, but I do recall one of the suggestions: "Why not keep the power source outside the chest cavity? Settle for temporary power sources and simply change batteries regularly. Two reserve batteries could be connected at all times to provide back-up power supply, providing a fail-safe system." *A sense of urgency has an enormous stimulating effect.*

3. *Ask Big Questions:* All players agree to investigate—and ask questions that will challenge the imagination. You will find this to be a most lucrative tip! One of our staff psychologists has said, "Almost all the problem people we see in our clinic have reached a frustration level of desperation because they don't ask big enough questions."

For centuries man sat under apple trees. Winds blew and apples fell. Apples would hit heads. For thousands of years the reaction in this situation had been predictable: Either man would get mad at the tree, the wind, or the apple, or he'd be hungry and wouldn't get mad—he'd just eat the apple, or he'd have other things on his mind and would quickly ignore the commonplace occurrence. Then, one day an apple fell on a certain man's head. What was his reaction? This time the special man, Isaac Newton, reacted differently. He asked a big question: "Why did the apple go down—and not up? Why did it *fall* and not *rise* like a feather in the wind?"

A big question, incredibly simple, unlocked creative thinking and resulted in the revelation of the law of gravity. Curiosity is the Mother of Creativity, just as Necessity is the Mother of Invention.

Here is another example. All radio stations in New Zealand were owned and operated by the government at one time. An acquaintance of mine, Jim Frankham, Jr., of Auckland, together with some of his dynamic young Possibility Thinking friends, decided the country would be vastly enriched if it also had privately owned and controlled commercial radio stations.

"Impossible!" they were told. "The government would never allow it."

The big question—How can we broadcast to the people of New Zealand without violating the law?

One night the fellows decided to play the Possibility Thinking Game. The upshot was a bright idea from one young lawyer. Place a radio transmitter on an ocean ship going to anchor twelve miles from shore and broadcast to the mainland. They had found the answer but they had no money to buy or charter a ship. Again they played the game. The result? They approached a wealthy ship owner who was sympathetic to the idea.

"I'll let you use one of my ships—free, on one condition," he offered. "If you succeed in pressuring the government to finally give in and allow you to operate legally on the mainland, then I get a directorship on the board."

"It's a deal," they chimed in unanimously.

Now another "impossible" problem loomed. To release the ship from the harbor a permit would be necessary from the minister of marine. Worse yet, the same official also served as the minister of broadcasting. They were sure he'd never approve the sailing. Since Jim and his friends were truly religious, they would not contemplate deception.

"Let's try anyway," one of the group suggested. "What do we have to lose?"

The government official listened to the young men's request. His response was incredible. Did they hear him right?

"I'll tell you what I will do," he said, "I'll let you sail. The truth is I have, as minister of broadcasting, been privately thinking that our country might be enriched if we allowed private commercial radio stations. But I can't even bring the subject up! If you actually commence broadcasting, and if you do a constructive job of it to the point that the people pressure my office to change our national policy, and permit private broadcasting—well, I won't block it."

This occurred several years ago. The ship sailed and the station went on the air in international waters. New Zealanders were astounded, then inspired, as they heard fresh and free voices on their radios. They responded. Pressure for private broadcasting mounted. Within two years, the government relented and licensed the first commercial station to operate in that country! Now there are four additional private broadcasting stations in operation.

Investigate! You'll find a way!

4. *Innovate:* Develop the skill of spotting success principles in related and—this is very important—*nonrelated* situations. Isolate these principles, relate them to your problem, assimilate them into your own situation, and you'll become an innovator!

This principle was used by Cyrus McCormick, having his hair cut. The barber used old-fashioned clippers. Why not use this sliding, slicing bar principle in a grain-cutting machine? he thought. The result? Hand cutting of oats was replaced by a new invention called the McCormick reaper.

Get in the habit of spotting and analyzing all successful operations. Find out why it works. Ask what positive principle is being employed. Ask if you can adopt it to other situations.

5. *Assume Success:* In playing the Possibility Thinking Game, you are not permitted to verbalize creativity-shattering sentences such as "It costs too much," "We can't afford it," "We don't have the time," "We don't have the team," "The law won't allow it."

If you suspect that problems with money, time, or personnel do exist, however, you play separate games that focus on these additional problems by asking, "Where and how can we get the money?" "Who do we need to get on the team?" "How can we solve the time problem?" "How do we go about getting the law changed?" "How can we cut the time and cost?"

Meanwhile, you must go on the assumption that every one of these problems will be solved. If the project, cause, dream, or goal is truly vital, you will not be blocked by apparent obstacles. You maneuver, reconnoiter, and explore.

You don't stop—you keep moving ahead, assuming that somehow a door will open, support will be forthcoming, solutions will be found, help will arrive, a way will be found.

If your cause is valid, assume that money problems will be solved as you move along. In playing your game, use this rule: Unlimited money is available. Think of the ideas that might surface if you knew that you could dip into millions of dollars to fund your project. Never allow lack of finances to repress thinking in the creative stage! If you come up with an exciting concept, money will flow toward you! Millions of dollars are added daily to savings accounts all over the world. This money is waiting, longing for great new investment opportunities.

Assume that laws can and will be changed. If there are existing laws prohibiting you from doing what you want to do, hire a Possibility Thinking lawyer, or contact your elected representatives.

Dr. William Brashears, of Fullerton, California, decided to build a beautiful shopping center over a strategic ten-acre parcel of land. This choice location was at a major crossroads. It was odd that no one had developed it before this time, for it was a commercial "natural." Investigation revealed the reason. A county flood control channel was planned to cut through its center. The law prohibited building over a flood control channel.

"Why not?" Bill asked. "Why couldn't a large underground tunnel be built to handle the water flow? With modern construction methods one could safely build over it."

He believed. He crusaded. He won! The law was changed. The Brashears Center today features a glistening twelve-story structure. Flowing harmlessly beneath it, inside a reinforced concrete tunnel, is the flood control channel.

Assume also that various details and difficulties can be handled by experts—financial, technical, political, legal, or psychological. Assume that in this vast world there's someone, somewhere, with the brains to help you succeed. Assume that you can enlist his help.

A few young fellows on the West Coast put together a new business and surprisingly succeeded in hiring a world-famed chemist. "I was looking for a change—something fresh, young, and challenging, and when these fellows approached me—well—I was struck by them," the esteemed researcher explained.

Assume that you'll be able to arrange or rearrange your time schedule to do what has to be done. If you are talking about a program that appears to need a five year period and you have only a year in which to do it—you don't give up. Assume that you will figure out a way to do it five times faster.

6. *Now draw close to God:* Let the Creative Mind of the universe inspire you. Wilma Todd was born with cerebral palsy and lives in a wheelchair. She belongs to a group of wheelchair friends who formed a bowling team. They call themselves Can Do Its.

"How in the world do you bowl?" I asked her.

"We wanted to bowl so much that we had a ramp built and let the ball roll down. It's loads of fun!" Wilma laughs, adding, "It's not your disabilities but your abilities that count." All it requires is faith. Someone said, "Faith is responsibility—my response to God's ability."

So play the Possibility Thinking Game and you'll discover, recover, or uncover an uncanny ability to be a really creative person. You'll be invited to problem-solving parties and be introduced with the words, "Now here's a fellow who will be able to figure out a way we can do it."

6

NOW—WIPE OUT FEAR OF FAILURE AND MOVE AHEAD

Remember that bar in the tiger cage? Recall how free you felt when you worked it loose?

Careful. Just when some exciting new possibility arises, you can expect that old enemy to return and try a comeback.

To succeed in becoming the person you want to be, eliminate once and for all the persistent problem called *Fear of Failure*.

You may have dreamed up solutions, you may have creative ideas, but until you wipe out Fear of Failure, your project will never get off the ground. Your goals will turn to shoals on which your best ideas will founder. Instead of boosting you, they'll bog you down. Goals inspire Possibility Thinkers to aspire. Goals tend to inspire fearful thinkers to expire.

This may explain why negative-thinking Sigmund Freud objected to goal setting. He saw the potential dangers. "Unfulfilled goals generate illness producing anxiety and frustration," he contended. It also explains why another Viennese psychiatrist, positive-thinking Viktor Frankl, insists on goal setting. He sees possibilities. "A lack of goals removes all meaning from living," he states.

The truth is both Freud and Frankl are right! The solution, however, is not to fear goals, but to wipe out *Fear* of Failure. The truth is that through Possibility Thinking you wipe failure out of your life. You do this when you turn failure from a negative into a positive force. You do it by redefining the meaning of failure.

Failure doesn't mean you are a failure. . . . *It does mean* you haven't succeeded yet.
Failure doesn't mean you have accomplished nothing. . . . *It does mean* you have learned something.

Failure doesn't mean you have been a fool. . . . *It does mean* you had a lot of faith.

Failure doesn't mean you've been disgraced. . . . *It does mean* you were willing to try.

Failure doesn't mean you don't have it. . . . *It does mean* you have to do something in a different way.

Failure doesn't mean you are inferior. . . . *It does mean* you are not perfect.

Failure doesn't mean you've wasted your life. . . . *It does mean* you have a reason to start afresh.

Failure doesn't mean you should give up. . . . *It does mean* you must try harder.

Failure doesn't mean you'll never make it. . . . *It does mean* it will take a little longer.

Failure doesn't mean God has abandoned you. . . . *It does mean* God has a better idea!

By this positive definition of failure, you truly eliminate failure as it is usually understood and defined by negative thinkers. Failure is never real failure if it becomes a guiding or strength-producing force! True failure is nothing more than a negative mental attitude. Got a bright idea? Afraid it might not be successful? Conquer your fear of failure by calling yourself a "researcher." Now *try*—and label your attempt an "experiment." Then failure is impossible! Researchers and experimenters cannot fail—they always succeed in testing an idea to find out if it will work or not!

Wash Fear Out of Your Thinking

One of two emotions will dominate and drive you—either faith or fear. Never surrender the leadership of your life to fear! The Bible is filled with commands to be courageous. Someone counted the "fear nots" in the Bible and discovered that there are 365 verses with the divine theme to fear not. One for every day of the year! Read a few of these calls to courage:

"Fear not for when you go through the waters they will not overflow you: when you go through the fire it will not consume you. For I am your God—I will be with you." (Isa. 33:1-2.)

"Be strong and of good courage. Be not afraid, neither be thou dismayed, for the Lord thy God is with thee whithersoever thou goest." (Josh 1:9.)

Negative Fear Is Abnormal

Since most, if not all, humans are inclined to fear at times, this does not mean that fear is normal and natural. The normal state of man is health. The abnormal state is sickness. Fear is not normal, in the sense that it does not come from God. It comes from the unbelieving mind of negative thinkers. The Bible teaches this clearly: "For God has not given us the spirit of fear: but the power of love, and of a sound mind." (2 Tim. 1:7.)

Dr. E. Stanley Jones, one of the most learned minds of this century, summed it up beautifully:

> I see that I am inwardly fashioned for faith and not for fear. Fear is not my native land; faith is. I am so made that worry and anxiety are sand in the machinery of life: faith is oil. I live better by faith and confidence than by fear and doubt and anxiety. In anxiety and worry my being is gasping for breath—these are not my native air. But if faith and confidence I breathe freely—these are my native air. A John Hopkins doctor says that "We do not know why it is that worriers die sooner than the non-worriers, but that is a fact." But I, who am simple of mind, think I know: we are inwardly constructed, in nerve and tissue, and brain cell and soul, for faith and not for fear. God made us that way. To live by worry is to live against reality.*

Fear—A Paralyzing Power

No force, no emotion is more paralyzing than fear. It stops a salesman about to make his call; the young man about to propose marriage; a job hunter about to seek an interview; an executive moments before he makes a decisive move; a seeker after truth about to commit his life to God.

In the whole, soridid, sorry spectacle of human fears,

---

*E. Stanley Jones, *Abundant Living* (Nashville, Tenn.: Abingdon Press).

none is more destructive and defeating than Fear of Failure. Eject this fear out of your life.

> Stop Your Fears
> before
> Your Fears Stop You!

Here's How

1. Expose your Fear of Failure to the light of truth. Fear thrives in darkness. Faith thrives in daylight. Throw the light of understanding on your Fear of Failure and you make the amazing discovery that you are not really afraid of failure after all. You think you are afraid of failure, but you are not. What you really fear is that if you fail, your friends and your peers will laugh at you or leave you. The fear of failure is, in fact, a fear of embarrassment or abandonment. But why fear abandonment? After all you are able to care for yourself.

Then why are you afraid? Because the fear of abandonment is a fear of the loss of your self-esteem. You fear disgrace. *So you are not really afraid of failure, you only think you are.* You are afraid that you'll lose your self-respect! Remind yourself that people never abandon the hard-trying loser. For years the New York Mets were the laughing stock of the baseball world. But their fans loved them in spite of that because they knew the team was trying to win. Finally, in 1969, the Mets won the World Series. The fans' faith had paid off.

Rats flee a sinking ship. Friends who leave because you failed aren't real friends. "A true friend," a sage once said, "is the person who steps in when the whole world steps out." The best people in the world run to the side of an honest loser and ask, "What can I do to help?" Admiring your spirit, they pat you on the back with the sincere compliment, "You're a good sport."

You'll truly love yourself when you see what wonderful friends you have. Remember that honest failure is no disgrace—lack of faith is the real shame. Cowardice is shameful.

If you don't try because you are afraid that you may have to work harder, sacrifice more, or get involved, that is ignoble! When you try again and again and demonstrate dedication, courage, faith, and self-sacrifice, you will attract a whole new set of real friends, those who give your self-respect a boost.

Being made in the image of God, man cannot stand to be shamed. Man's nature demands that he be treated with dignity. Fear of Failure is a self-contrived defense mechanism subconsciously fabricated to shelter an insecure ego from moving ahead in a risky and potentially embarrassing experience.

2. You decide to build self-dignity by ignoring your so-called Fear of Failure and you develop amazing insight and discover that Fear of Failure does not promote or protect self-respect. Actually this fear is a contraceptive that prevents a self-respect. Suppose you have a great idea, but having surrendered to Fear of Failure, you let the golden opportunity pass you by. You remain safe from fear of embarrassment but now you are bored. *Boredom doesn't build self-esteem.* What does boredom do? It gives you loads of time to think, "It might have worked."

To quote John Greenleaf Whittier:

> For of all sad words of tongue or pen,
> The saddest are these: "It might have been."

You grow old, collecting and nursing a multitude of regrets. Why didn't I do this? Why didn't I do that? Why didn't I buy it when I had a chance? To further depress yourself, you may see someone else seizing the same opportunity. They are successful and you become jealous. The pangs of further jealousy will make you more bitter and inspire further negative thoughts and actions. Thus Fear of Failure does not protect your self-respect—it prevents and aborts it. If you heed your fears you'll die never knowing what a great person you might have been.

3. Remind yourself that there is no progress without risk. Not until you have a failure can you be sure you aimed high enough. Success is making the most of the op-

NOW—WIPE OUT FEAR OF FAILURE AND MOVE AHEAD 79

portunity God has given you. Failure is failing to make the most of the gifts and lifts that God offers you.

James Bryant Conant, the distinguished president of Harvard, said, "Behold the turtle—he makes progress only when he sticks his neck out." British Foreign Secretary Lord Halifax put it in these words: "He that leaveth nothing to chance will do few things ill, but he will do few things." And Ben Franklin made the same point: "The man who does things makes many mistakes, but he doesn't make the biggest mistake of all—doing nothing."

If you are not facing some risks *now,* you are not growing or progressing. You are standing still or you are retrogressing.

4. Remind yourself that if you allow this fear to control you, you will be doomed to a dull, lifeless, adventureless existence.

5. Banish perfectionism from your mind. Fear of Failure thrives in the overly idealized thinking of the perfectionist mentality.

> It's Better to Do
> Something Imperfectly
> Than to Do Nothing
> Perfectly

Perfectionism, also, is a fear of rejection. You fear that failure will expose you as an imperfect person. Think realistically—and realize no one is perfect. And no intelligent person expects you to be perfect. Beautiful and good people will never reject you when your imperfection is exposed by failure. It may just prove that you're a human being. Every individual is a failure in some way, at some time, on some level. Remember: "To err is human, to forgive is divine."

In the final analysis people will accept or reject you not for what you do—but for what kind of person you are.

6. Realize that failure is never final and total. Many men and women have had a failed marriage that ended in di-

vorce and then went on to a second successful marriage! You may fail in one business venture and become successful in another.

Impossibility Thinkers are deceitful masters of extreme, irresponsible, negative statements: "I'm all washed up." "I've had it." "I'll never amount to anything." "I'm a total washout." "I'm finished." *Every one of these statements is an exaggerated untruth!* Never, never talk or think in this way.

Dr. Smiley Blanton, one of the most esteemed psychiatrists of the century, once said to his colleague, Norman Vincent Peale, "I have been a psychiatrist for almost forty years and if there is one thing that is clear to me it is this: *There are vast undamaged areas in every human life* if only they could be discovered and if only the person could be made to believe it and rebuild on it. No person is a hopeless case."

He went on to explain: "Freud saw this and wrote, 'It seems like even the most psychotic cases report that there are moments when they watch their own sick self move along outside of themselves and they almost are like a spectator watching the whole tragic tragedy unfold.'"

Richard Lemon in an article entitled "The Uncertain Science" tells about an occurrence at a mental hospital in a Paris suburb during the Second World War. The institution housed 154 cases that were judged by the best psychiatrists to be hopelessly insane. One dark night the invading armies of liberation shelled the walls of the hospital. In the ensuing confusion all 154 escaped. Many years later when they finally traced down each of those patients, they were amazed to find that 86 out of the 154 had completely recovered and were living perfectly normal lives. Remember: There is no such thing as a total failure this side of hell!

7. "So what's real failure?" you ask yourself at this point. The answer comes clear. Real failure is to fail as a person. To yield to cowardice in the face of an urgent but risky venture. To fearfully retreat from a high call to noble duty because you can see the possibility of imperfection in your performance of that duty.

To be more concerned about protecting your pride from an embarrassing failure than about promoting a wonderful and worthy cause. To demote faith from the leadership of your future life and promote fear to a power-base position of authority over your destiny. This is real failure as a person.

8. Now suffocate your fears. Isolate yourself from those who would tell you, "It can't be done," "It'll never work," "Somebody else tried it and failed," "It's never been done before."

Isolate yourself from such destructive, negative forces. Isolate yourself against the persons who generate depressing, discouraging vibrations. Suffocate your fears. Deprive them of their life support systems.

9. Now join the N.F.A. Club. That's the Never Fear Again Club. How do you get in this club? Develop a strong personal faith in God. The deeply religious person is unflappable. A distinguished, elderly gentleman of my acquaintance puts it this way: "The man who watches over me never makes any mistakes."

A student who is taking a most challenging college course tells me he writes his fears on a piece of paper, wraps them in a circle, and pierces the paper with an arrow that represents Jesus Christ.

One of the boldest of American businessmen was the late Robert LeTourneau. He shared the secret of his daring in this simple thought: "God is my partner. How could you ever be afraid if you had a partner like that?"

"Every time I go before the cameras, or walk on stage, I pray, 'Use me, Lord, use me,' " my friend Doris Day told me. She added "There's always the danger in my business that one personalizes his work. When I came to see myself as a channel for God to use, I stopped worrying about possible goofs I might make."

Show me a person with a consuming dream coupled with a deep unshakable faith and I'll show you a champion mountain mover. He's positive he'll succeed. He believes the Bible verse "In everything you do put God first and He will crown your efforts with success." (Prov. 3:6.)

Ethel Waters has this slogan: "God don't sponsor no flops."

Superstrength Can Be Yours

Vincent H. Gaddis tells several stories of superhuman strength that has miraculously saved lives:*

Twelve-year-old Robert Heitsche was playing on a building construction site in West Covina, California, one afternoon in 1965 when he was buried under a half ton of steel scaffolding and bricks. The cries of Robert's playmates brought Patrolman Clint Collins, twenty-eight, to the scene. The 155-pound officer stooped and with one quick motion raised the entire mass of scaffolding with its burden of bricks.

"It was just the sight of that little guy's hand sticking out through the steel and bricks that got me," Collins said. "At that moment I would have tried crashing through a brick wall to help." . . .

On a November morning in 1964 the frame of a nine-seat station wagon was moving slowly along the final assembly line at the Fisher Body Company plant in Flint, Michigan. The frame was mounted on a steel conveyor truck. The weight of the frame and truck was well over a ton.

Victor W. Howell, twenty-one, was standing beside the assembly line. He waited until the frame of a car ahead of the station wagon had passed him, then leaned over to check an equipment order tag.

Suddenly his foot slipped, and he lost his balance and fell. As he rolled out of the way, his foot was caught in the conveyor at a point where it dipped below the floor's surface. He was trapped, helpless. The truck with its heavy frame was now only inches away. Within seconds his leg would be crushed to pulp. . . .

Charles J. McClendon, a relief man in another part of the plant, appeared at the scene just as Howell screamed for help. McClendon, forty-eight, was five feet, ten inches in height, and weighed 205 pounds. He was a husky man, but now he became a superhuman.

"I remember I had my back to the truck and frame with my hands gripped under the truck," he said later. "I didn't know what to do, and then it was as if there was a voice inside me and it said, 'Lift it off there!' And somehow I did it. . . .

At Columbus, Ohio, in 1966, Carolyn Horn, an eighteen-year-old girl who weighed less than a hundred pounds, moved a forty-foot-long, one-foot-thick tree limb a distance of about four feet at one end to rescue a cousin pinned beneath it. . . .

Mrs. Gene Perryman, twenty-five, was standing on the back porch of her Jasper County, South Carolina, home on October 1, 1965, holding her baby. Her two older children,

*Vincent H. Gaddis, *Courage in Crisis* (New York: Hawthorn, 1973).

NOW—WIPE OUT FEAR OF FAILURE AND MOVE AHEAD 83

Andy, eight, and Vicki, nine, were out in front of the house waiting for the school bus.

She heard Vicki scream, and her daughter's cry was followed by the squeal of automobile brakes. Placing the baby in a crib on the porch, she ran around the house to the highway. Andy had been struck by a car and dragged 160 feet before the driver could bring his sedan to a stop. The boy was wedged between a rear wheel and the gasoline tank beneath the car.

"I'm not sure how I did it," Mrs. Perryman told newsmen afterward. "It happened so quickly. But I knew I had to get my boy out. He was pinned beneath the gas tank, and I was afraid it would catch fire."

Seizing the rear bumper of the car, Mrs. Perryman raised the vehicle and shoved it until it rolled off her son and into a ditch. Andy was taken to Candler Hospital in Savannah where he was later reported in good condition. The car weighed nineteen hundred pounds. Mrs. Perryman was a small woman, just under five feet in height, and she weighed ninety-eight pounds.

"If it had been your child," she said, "you would have found the strength as I did." . . .

What is the source of this amazing energy? . . .

It is now known that a chemical called adenosine triphosphate (ATP) is responsible for our energy. When activated by impulses from the brain, ATP provides power to muscles in a complex twenty-stage chemical reaction almost explosive in effect.

The following demonstration of superstrength is one of the most incredible ever recorded:*

The time was shortly before midnight on February 18, 1952, and the place was ten miles north of Houston, Texas. Roy Gaby was returning to Houston from Waco, driving a large fourteen-wheel truck-trailer, when a car driven by an apparently intoxicated man swung onto the highway from a side road without stopping. Gaby swerved to avoid a collision, lost control, and the front of the truck crashed into a huge oak tree. The trailer piled on top of the telescoped cab, trapping Gaby in the twisted wreckage.

Gaby's body was doubled up beneath the crushed top of the cab. His feet were pinned between the twisted clutch and brake pedals, and the steering wheel was jammed against his waist. On both sides of the cab the doors were crumpled tight within their bent frames. The engine had been rammed back into the cab.

"First we hooked the wrecker to the front of the mashed-in engine with the idea of moving it out far enough to free

*Ibid.

the victim," Officer Henry told reporters later. "It didn't budge. Next we attached a truck to the front of the wrecker for more power. Nothing happened. Then we hooked two more trucks to the rear of the trailer to pull it in the opposite direction and jerk the wreckage apart. It didn't work."

As the engines of the wrecker and the three trucks roared and tugged fruitlessly, a spectator suddenly screamed: "She's on fire! My God! He's going to be burned alive!" Small flames appeared from beneath the cab and began licking their way along the floor. . . .

Truckers and motorists went to work on the crumpled doors, pounding with hammers and twisting and prying with crowbars. But the doors could not be budged.

"I've never seen a sight more terrible," Henry said. "I felt like praying for a miracle. The fire had reached the cab floor under the victim. By the time fire trucks and cutting torches arrived, it would be too late. And then this stranger, this husky black man, came up to me and asked if he could help. I shook my head. If three big trucks and a heavy-duty wrecker couldn't open that cab, nobody could help."

What happened next will never be forgotten by anyone who witnessed it.

Walking over to the cab, the Negro seized the door that had resisted hammers and wrecking bars and wrenched it off. Tossing the door aside, he ripped out the burning floor mat and with his bare hands beat out the flames around Gaby's feet. Reaching into the cab, he grabbed the steering column and bent it forward away from Gaby's waist. Next, with one hand on the clutch and the other on the brake pedal, he forced them apart and released the victim's feet. . . .

As the awe-stricken spectators stood frozen, the stranger, crawling on his knees, squeezed into the cab, bending aside crumpled metal that barred his movements. Finally he had wormed his way far enough to place himself in a position with his feet flat on the floor, his head down, and his neck and shoulders wedged tightly against the caved-in roof. His body stiffened under the strain as he exerted all his strength upward, his tensed muscles bulging against his sweat-drenched shirt.

There was a sudden, rippling sound as the metal gave way. Glaring at the flames with hate-filled eyes, the black man held the top up as Deputy Henry and several truckers quickly removed Gaby from the cab.

I would add, "A person doesn't know what he can do until God inspires him." For when the God impulse stirs the brain, not only is ATP released—All Types of Power to succeed are released!"

NOW—WIPE OUT FEAR OF FAILURE AND MOVE AHEAD 85

Turn Fear from a Negative into a Positive Force

If after reading the examples given above you still sense an inclination to fear that you cannot eliminate—then sublimate it! Make your fears work for you—not against you.

"I couldn't possibly live without the unknown in front of me," says Pierre Boulez, music director of the New York Philharmonic. This emotion you tend to call fear will be relabeled "mysteries of the future." So you begin to turn your fears into a positive force to motivate you:

> *Fear not* that you might fall. . . . *Fear rather* that you will never succeed.
> *Fear not* that you might be hurt. . . . *Fear rather* that you might never grow.
> *Fear not* that you might love and lose. . . . *Fear rather* that you might never love at all.
> *Fear not* that man might laugh at your mistakes. . . . *Fear rather* that God will address you "O ye of little faith."
> *Fear not* that you might fall again. . . . *Fear rather* that you might have made it the next time.

Ready? Up with the big idea. Get set to start. Risky? Good! It's your chance to live in the dimension of faith. Oscar Wilde said, "An idea that isn't dangerous is hardly worth calling an idea."

My friend Fred Jarvis writes simple lines, but they are telling! " 'Tis not your failure but low aim that is the crime and awful shame. Aim right. Aim high and raise your goal. With God plan big. With God plan bold."

7

WINNING STARTS WITH BEGINNING

What's holding you back? By now you know there is:

A goal you should be pursuing;
A dream you should be launching;
A plan you should be executing;
A project you should be starting;
A possibility you should be exploring;
An opportunity you should be grabbing;
An idea you should be working;
A problem you should be tackling;
A decision you should be making.

Now it's time to solve another tough problem: How To Begin.

At the age of fifty-nine he was an old, fat, flabby-fleshed high school janitor. He felt he was "over the hill."

"You can be the person you want to be. Visualize, organize, actualize, and realize," he heard his minister say one Sunday. "Just get started," the pastor concluded, pausing before he bellowed the last word, "TODAY!"

All his life Walt Frederick had bemoaned the fact that he was not athletic and in poor physical shape. Now the miracle of faith happened. He dared to believe he could become a physically fit athlete! He started by going on a controlled diet. Then he began to jog. One year later he was running two miles a day. He increased it to four miles every morning and an additional four miles at night. By the time he was sixty-one he was slim and trim, in better condition than he'd been in his whole life including his teenage years. Now he was running one hundred miles every week.

I'll never forget the morning he met me after a church service. "Guess where I'm going next week, Rev.?" he asked. His eyes sparkled with youthful enthusiasm. Before I could answer, he told me, "I'm flying to Boston. I'm going to run in the Boston Marathon—that's twenty-eight miles and three hundred and sixty-five yards." And off he ran! Over a thousand runners started that race. Only a fraction of them finished. Walt Frederick was among the finishers. Four years after, he had a wall filled with medals and trophies. He is nationally known for his record-breaking runs.

"What's the biggest problem you faced in these years?" I asked him. Without a moment's hesitation he answered, "I can answer that in one word, my biggest problem *was* and *is* inertia."

I believed it then—I believe it now—that's my biggest problem—and *yours!*

Four Kinds of People—Which Kind Are You?

Take a look now at four kinds of people:

1. *No-No Persons:* They never start. No wonder they never succeed. They always have an excuse for the lack of achievement. One athletic director had so many problems with negative thinkers that he decided to mimeograph copies of an alibi sheet. It began with these words:

"This list is intended to simplify the problem of selecting the proper alibi to suit the occasion. While some athletes are so bad that they don't need an alibi, most will at some time be in need of some explanation to account for some performance and the following hand check list may prove helpful:"

ate too much
weak from lack of nourishment
not enough time to warm up

warmed up too much
overtrained
not enough training
not enough sleep
too much sleep
need wheat germ oil
need yogurt
not enough weight lifting
too much weight lifting
I'm building up slowly for four years from now

I didn't think
I thought too much
poor judges
poor starter
poor track
footing too hard
footing too soft
too warm
too cold
shin splints
blisters
spikes too short
spikes too long
I didn't have red shoes
forgot to bring shoes
cramp in leg

I don't want to improve too rapidly
worried about studies
worried about finances
girlfriend unfriendly last night
girlfriend too friendly last night

snowblindness
got lost
thought there was another lap to go
thought the race ended a lap sooner than it did
can't run when I'm behind
can't run when I'm ahead
can't run
too much competition
too many meets
cheap meals
I wanted to see what the other place medals were like

too many people were depending on me
nobody cared about my performance
I don't like organized athletics

cramp in ———
didn't feel like running
I have emotional problems
chicken
my coach is a———
cold feet
thought I was having a heart attack

I only run for the exercise
I couldn't be excited about the race
I was overanxious
I heard we weren't getting a meal after the meet
my coach is an American and he does not understand foreign athletes
my coach is a foreigner and he does not understand American athletes
looking forward to the indoor season
looking forward to the outdoor season
we didn't train this way in junior high school
I don't want to be too successful

2. *Yo-Yo Persons:* They're up and down, in and out, hot and cold, dreamers and delayers.

3. *Blow-Blow Persons:* They think big, talk big, but back off just when they should move ahead.

4. *Go-Go Persons:* They think big, talk big, perform big! They put their reputation on the line with public announcements, "I'm going to win!" And they surge ahead to success. They will not be labeled "a big breeze."

One of the most impressive lessons I ever learned was as a guest in the home of W. Clement Stone, a self-made centi-millionaire, prominent philanthropist, successful author, and one of the greatest positive thinkers who ever lived. At dinner Clem Stone, Dr. Karl Menninger, and I were discussing "great concepts."

I said, "To my mind faith is the greatest concept."

Clem Stone said, "I think there is something more important than believing. Action! The world is full of dreamers, there aren't enough who will move ahead and begin to take concrete steps to actualize their visions."

Stop Making Excuses for Not Starting!

Procrastination is your greatest enemy. Delays will turn pregnant opportunities into hollow possibilities. If you don't have the faith to move ahead NOW, don't be surprised when that bigger believer appears and launches your idea successfully. You'll moan and groan saying, "I thought about doing that—why didn't I?"

Goethe wrote: "Lose this day loitering, twill be the same story tomorrow and the next more dilatory. Indecision brings its own delays and days are lost lamenting over day. Action—there is courage, magic in it. Anything you can do, or think you can, begin it. Once started, the mind grows heated. Begin the job and the work will be completed."

What's holding you back?

1. *Hang-ups?* Let's look at some of these hang-ups that have become classic excuses for our inertia.

"I'M TOO OLD."

Is seventy-seven years of age too old to begin a new life? If you're a negative thinker hung up on the "old-age prejudice," you'll consider yourself too close to the grave to start anything new. If you're a Possibility Thinker, you'll assume you have another ten to twenty years of life left. In 1972 Frieda Schulze celebrated, at the age of eighty-seven, her escape from East Berlin ten years before. At the age of seventy-seven she took the plunge toward a new life.

"I still shudder a bit when I think about it," Frau Schulze said as she recalled the incident that made newspaper headlines around the world in 1962. "But it was worth it . . . I couldn't stand their politics," she added, shaking a gnarled finger for emphasis.

When the East German communists built their wall across Berlin on August 13, 1961, Frau Schulze lived on the ground floor of an apartment house smack on the border at Bernauerstrasse in Berlin's Wedding District. The sidewalk was in West Berlin but the house belonged to the East.

As East German police and troops uncoiled barbed wire,

hundreds of people on the East side of Bernauerstrasse, which became known as the saddest street in the world, threw a few belongings out of windows and escaped. The East Germans then bricked up ground floor windows and moved the remaining residents into upper-level apartments vacated by those who had escaped.

"They moved me up, too, and when I got to the new place I sat there as if I were paralyzed," Frau Schulze said. "I had no light in the apartment, but that wasn't necessary because there were so many searchlights outside. It was a terrible light, and I sat right in the middle."

Frau Schulze's sleep was often interrupted by the sound of shots aimed at escaping refugees, the horns and sirens of fire engines and ambulances, and the voices of West Berliners shouting encouragement to residents beyond the wall or vulgarities at East German guards.

"Finally I could not stand it anymore, and on September 23 I decided to escape. I tied a rope to my biggest armchair and I planned to let myself down on it. I lay awake all night thinking about it and the next morning I was ready to do everything . . . I was going to jump," the white-haired, slightly built woman remembered. "I went to the bathroom and washed myself. I was going to be clean when I left my home."

What happened next was captured in newsphotos that were transmitted around the world. Frau Schulze climbed onto the windowsill. The moment she was spotted by West Berlin police officers, the fire brigade was called. A net was spread fifteen feet below her. In her arms she clutched her cat.

"The people started yelling 'Grandma, jump,' over and over, and I guess the noise alerted the VOPO's (Communist People's Police). I heard them kick in the door of the apartment and two of them came to the window and tried to pull me back."

The West Berliners on the sidewalk saw her plight. A young man climbed on the windowsill of the ground floor. Held by policemen, he reached up and grabbed Frau Schulze's leg and began pulling her down while a communist police officer pulled one arm upward. The other arm still held the cat.

"I threw the cat into the net, and then I jumped."

The crowd roared with joy and applauded Frau Schulze's escape. She was lucky, injuring her hip only slightly.

The truth is many people will—in the next twenty-five years—live to be a hundred! Scientists are prolonging life. Expect to live to be a hundred. Now then, you're still pretty young today, aren't you?

Let's look at another hang-up:

"I'M THE VICTIM OF RACIAL PREJUDICE."

Many people are indeed victims of racial prejudice all over the world. Still in every country where racism exists you will find those exceptional individuals who smash the race barrier and succeed in spite of this problem. If you live in a community where racial prejudice does, in fact, exist, don't use this as an excuse to keep from trying. Use it as a challenge to hurdle over the obstacle!

"I DON'T HAVE A GOOD EDUCATION."

Then get one! In most states of the United States you can go to night school and earn a high school diploma and a college degree. A poor education is no longer a valid excuse for not moving ahead, at any age.

"I DON'T HAVE ANY MONEY."

Then go out and earn it, save it, or borrow it. Where there's a will, there's a way. Start small, build your savings, scrimp and save, and you'll be astonished at how the way will become clear.

"You have not because you ask not," the Bible says. Have you asked everyone you can think of to help you bankroll your idea? Or have you held back because you're too embarrassed to ask for a loan? Then don't ask for a loan—ask your friend to "rent" you some money. Offer to pay him "higher rent" than his present savings account is paying him! You'll be doing him a real favor.

2. *Bang-ups?* Is that what's holding you back? Are old hurts, old defeats, and old setbacks haunting, holding, and hurting you?

"I'll never get married again."

"I'll never trust anyone again."

"I'll never believe in God again."

"I'll never go into business again."

"I've been burned once—never again!"

If you think this way then you have allowed past unfortunate incidents to move in and dominate you. Don't let bad memories manipulate you. A friend, Don Herbert, has had his share of human heartache. When I called to offer my sympathy on the loss of his father he said, "Well, we just look ahead—you can't get far looking in the rearview mirror."

When the English historian Thomas Carlyle finished his many thousands of pages of manuscript on the French Revolution, he gave it to his neighbor John Stuart Mill to read. Several days later, looking pale and nervous, Mill came to Carlyle's home. Mill's maid had used the manuscript to start a fire. Carlyle was in a frenzy for days. Two years of labor lost; he could never muster the energy to write again. Then one day he saw a mason building a long, large wall, laying one brick at a time. This sight inspired him. He decided to start over. "I'll just write one page today—then one page at a time," he said. He started then and slowly went on to finish the work that he felt was better than the first manuscript.

3. *Gang-ups?* Are they dragging you down to keep you from launching out? Is competition building up? Are your business enemies ganging up on you? A positive mental attitude is your only answer.

A Chinese merchant operated a small store in the middle of a city block. One day a huge chain started construction of a store on one corner of the block while a giant department store began to arise on the other corner. He was crushed between two enormous competitors. The day came when both new stores were ready to open their doors. Both companies strung huge banners that read "Grand Opening Sale." What did the little man in the middle do? He hung a sign over his doorway reading "Main Entrance."

4. *Rang-ups?* Are they holding you back? Have you rung up so many accomplishments, victories, and achievements that you're tired and you've decided to retire? Do you look at the trophies, the awards, and the prizes of yesterday and lean on these laurels? "I've gone down the hill ever since I won the highest award the company can give," a salesman reported. "I guess I was trying to prove something to someone and now I don't seem to care anymore."

How do you overcome this? Try letting God stimulate you. Read this Bible verse over and over again: "Forgetting those things that are behind, and reaching forth to those things that are before, I press toward the mark for The Prize of the High Calling of God." (Phil. 3:13-14.)

Remind yourself that ease will always lead to disease. As soon as you stop exercising your body the youthful muscles will lose their power. Either use—or lose—your inner powers. Avoid the kill that comes from the standstill. If you want to stay on the bicycle of life you have to keep pedaling—or you will fall.

A friend who was gravely injured in an accident wanted to give up. "When I had painfully regained enough power to walk with crutches I was tired of struggling through the torture of physical therapy until my therapist warned me, 'You'll lose whatever you've gained if you don't keep trying to improve.' I have since learned that this is a universal principle of life!"

> There Is No Gain without Pain

Now—Use These Self-motivators to Get Yourself Moving

1. Add up the rewards of beginning and the cost of neglecting to begin. Mentally add up all of the values, benefits, and rewards that will accrue to you and to others if you accomplish what you have been dreaming about. Then, add up all of the losses you will suffer if you don't get started.

We all call her "Grandma Finley." She's eighty-four years old. I met her on a Pacific cruise. She attracted so much attention that a newspaperman interviewed her. "Will this be your last cruise, Mrs. Finley?" she was asked.

"Goodness no!" she snapped. "I'm a member of a worldwide club. the CMT—Can't Miss a Thing. That's our motto." And laughing she added, "Anyway, I've got no pockets in my shroud. When this tour is over I will sell some more real estate, make a nickel, and buy another ticket."

"But doesn't an old person of your age have problems

traveling?" the twenty-four-year-old newspaperman questioned.

"Of course," Grandma answered. "But so do the kids! I really don't worry. People are so helpful. Like the time I was ashore in Lapland buying a doll for my collection. Someone said the Russian border was close, so off I went to get a look at Russia and when I got back to the wharf the ship had its walkways up and was starting to move. I didn't know what to do. Before I had a chance to think, two brawny fishermen picked me up and hurled me bodily through an open door in the ship's side. My, my, my, I wouldn't have let them do that if they had asked."

2. Generate a sense of urgency. Larry Regan, while coach of the Los Angeles Kings, explained two outstanding victories. "At the key moments," the National Hockey League coach said, "the men played with a sense of urgency—you can't beat that."

Look at your calendar. You're not getting any younger. You'll probably never be in better health than you are today. A year from now you may wish you had started today! Is time getting away from you? Is life passing you by? Will it be easier—or cheaper—if you wait another week, or month, or year?

Build a sense of urgency into your thinking and get going! "Winter is coming." "A test is coming up." "Relatives are coming to visit." "I'll soon be too old to go." "The inspector will be dropping around." "The boss will be calling for a report." "I'll have to step on the scale in the doctor's office next month."

Average people produce under pressures generated by events, circumstances, or other persons who control their life in part or in whole. Exceptional persons produce under urgent pressures they have deliberately generated themselves!

So they first sign a contract to deliver by a certain date; then they release a public announcement of their intention to produce. So they commit themselves in such a way that they have to go ahead with it! (A word of caution: At the early stage announce your plans only to *trusted friends* and *proven Possibility Thinkers*. Beware of Impossibility Thinkers. Protect your precious plan from the deadly infection of Impossibility Thinking. Newborn babies must be sheltered until they have developed immunity to a new germ-infected environment.)

3. Make out a schelule—now. Schedule planning sessions, decision-making meetings, and problem-solving meetings. Write them on your personal calendar. By doing this you insure your future time. You will succeed if you will only make time to work your plan. Remind yourself that you will certainly fail if you do not block out the time. Nothing will happen unless you mark it on your calendar NOW!

Now break up your dream into time stages. Mark on your calendar the beginning and the concluding date of the planning stage, the launching stage, the problem-solving stages, and the celebration of success date! Aim at a "special" day like Christmas or New Years or your next birthday. Then promise yourself a reward on that day. A new suit of clothes, a trip, a special dinner in your favorite restaurant. Now tell yourself, "I've got a great thing going—I must not stop it!"

> The Hardest Part of
> Any Job
> Is Getting Started

4. Now begin to build your base. Slowly, solidly, sincerely. "If you have faith you can accomplish anything," Jesus said. But He did not say that you could do it all at once.

A man who had read *Move Ahead with Possibility Thinking* wanted to establish a national sales organization (and he could have). He borrowed two hundred thousand dollars in order to rent offices in major cities before he had built a local base. Since there was no money coming in from any one base, he quickly went bankrupt.

Be willing to build slowly, surely, solidly. Start small. When your first stage is successful, expand to the second stage. Keep growing.

Visitors to the Garden Grove Community Church are inspired and impressed by the enormous church plant located on twenty-two acres. I often have to explain, "We made a master plan before we started. What you see now was built in nine separate construction operations over a period of seventeen years."

Remember. Start Small. Build strong. Keep growing—that's the way the pyramids were built. And that's the way to reach the top. Ignore the base-building principle and you can move too far too fast until you are over your head!

5. Now multiply the levels of your motivation. I once had a bad fall from a ladder that hospitalized me. Though I recovered full health, I got out of the self-disciplined habit of walking two miles every day. To get going again was unbelievably difficult. I told myself, "If I walk, it will keep my heart healthy." But I didn't get started. So I added, "Walking will give me a trimmer figure and reduce that bulging waistline!" Still I didn't move. So I added, "If I walk two miles every day, I will stay young for a long time." I recalled my grandfather who lived to be ninety-six. He took long walks every day. I still couldn't get going, so I added another level of motivation: "If I walk every day and continue to do so, I'll retain youthful posture all my life." That did it. That final reason for walking, on top of the other reasons, finally brought enough weight to bear and caused it to sink into that deep level of consciousness where action is triggered! It got me going. Keep adding purposeful motivating reasons.

6. Call for help! On the second day of my new walking program I was reluctant to start out. I asked my son to walk with me and make me go. He did! It was the added boost I needed. Ask someone to help you begin. Ask a friend or relative to give you a push.

7. Use your mind. Don't wait until you feel like doing it. You won't feel like it until you're involved. Professional writers don't sit and wait for an inspiration. They make themselves start to write. Then the ideas come.

> # Use Your Head and Your Heart Will Follow

It's amazing how often inspiration comes through perspiration. When I am ready to write a book, I sit down at the typewriter and insert a sheet of paper. Then I type the title. That title may change a dozen times before publication but I choose a title. Then I type "By Robert H. Schuller." I then type on another sheet of paper "Other Books by Robert H. Schuller," and I list them. That helps me believe that I have successfully written books before and motivates me to begin. I then write the dedication. I put these three pages in a loose leaf binder. I'm on my way. Now I'm really enthusiastic about the project.

8. Don't wait to start until you see solutions to every problem. High achievers spot rich opportunities swiftly, make big decisions quickly, then move into action immediately. Slow movers are low achievers. By the time they're sure they can solve all problems, the opportunity has passed. Some "possibilitarian" has moved in and grabbed the opportunity from him. Opportunities don't wait for slow-thinking people.

Start now. Solve the problems later. What will you do when you run into a seemingly unsolvable difficulty? You'll invent a solution!

Fred Hostrop, a friend of mine writes:

> For years I suffered from acromegaly, which is caused by a tumor on my pituitary gland. This makes my pituitary gland over-active, which in turn causes me to grow abnormally large. I'm 73 years old and still growing! My skeleton is larger than normal. My tongue is so big, I can't speak over the phone. It has pushed my lower teeth out, and I don't have a good bite. I have to eat slowly and carefully, or I'll bite my tongue! I have severe backaches and headaches several hours each day and night. I cannot pick up anything on the floor or ground (can't bend over that far). Because I have poor equilibrium I cannot stand in any one place or

walk safely without two canes. I cannot walk more than about 200 feet without collapsing. Although my eyesight is excellent, I cannot keep my heavy eyelids open long enough to drive safely more than two miles.

Rev. Schuller, the above description of how acromegaly has affected me may sound like negative thinking. But instead of saying, 'I can't do this,' thinking positively I say to myself, 'What can I do about this situation I'm in?'

I've done many things. I'll give you only a few illustrations: We live on a large corner lot. The only practical way to water the parkway between the sidewalk and street curb is to water it by hand. About one hour's work. Because my back muscles are not strong enough to support my heavy skeleton, this was a job I dreaded. Enclosed snapshot shows how I water in a seated position on my 'water vehicle' with four casters under it, propelling myself backward comfortably, due to thinking positively!

Although I cannot play golf anymore on the golf course, I can still enjoy practicing in our yard. Enclosed pictures show another invention by positive-thinking-Hostrop which will pick up the golf ball off the ground and set it on the tee—hurrah! I also use it to pick up litter in our yard every day."

There's Always a Way When You Really Try

We have several walnut trees on our church grounds. California crows love the meat of the walnut. How can a crow crack a walnut to get at the meat? Imagine if you were a crow—how would you do it? The crows have figured out a way. They pick the walnut up in their bills, fly high over our church parking lot, and let the nuts fall on the hard surface! The walnuts crack—and the clever birds swoop down and eat the meat! If a crow's brain can find a solution to its problem, surely you'll be able to solve yours.

9. Yield to positive impulses when they arise. As strongly as you resist negative impulses to action, act strongly and promptly to positive ideas. Be positively impulsive.

Some years ago I was about to attend the World Psychiatric Conference in Madrid. I had been studying Spanish history and was curious about several recent incidents. "If only I could get an opportunity to corner Francisco Franco and ask him face to face about three things," I thought.

It was a great idea—but it seemed unrealistic; however, I decided to practice what I preached and *try*. I yielded to that positive impulse, picked up the telephone, called my congressman's office, and asked for assistance. That single call got me and several others involved in a major project —like a snowball rolling down a hill, and it hasn't stopped yet.

"It's impossible, Dr. Schuller," my congressman answered in a letter. "My aides tell me that Franco has never agreed to be interviewed by a Protestant minister. If you could present yourself as a secular author—maybe."

"I can't be dishonest," I answered, "Please try another way."

I left for Amsterdam and had no further word until I arrived in Paris and found a cable awaiting me. The message was brief and to the point: "General Francisco Franco agrees to see you at noon 22nd of August, La Corona, Spain." It ended with two beautiful words, "Good luck." One simple telephone call had started the project and it then rolled along on self-generating momentum that gathered steam and breakthrough power.

Someone once said to me, "Life is too short to do what we want to do." I answered, "Oh no it's not—not if you start on time!"

Wake up! Come alive! Snap the cords of laziness! Break the chains of lethargy! "It is high time to awake out of sleep." (Rom. 13:11.) "Truly, *now*, is the right time—*now* is the day of salvation." (2 Cor. 6:2.) "This is the day." (Pss. 118:24.)

Make up your mind to ACT NOW! Escape from the prison of inertia! DO IT NOW! Take some action NOW— telephone, write a letter, do something! Move! Act! Start! Begin! Get Going! NOW!

Shake up the negative thoughts. Shake all impossibility thoughts out of your mind! Shake them out! "Quit you like men—be strong." (1 Cor. 16:13.)

Break up the obstacles. Shatter the barriers. You can like making a doorway in the great wall of China. How? Remove one stone at a time. Break your biggest problems into small, workable pieces.

Take up the crowning accomplishment that is your destiny! You'll walk away with honors. People will respect and admire you. God will bless you. How happy you will be! You'll become the person you always wanted to be. Start acting like a Possibility Thinker—NOW!

If your biggest obstacle is getting started—you can eliminate that! Right now!

8

ENTHUSIASM—THIS POWER WILL PUT YOU IN ORBIT

Enthusiasm is the propellant power that will take you from a slow lift-off, into a steady, upward surge. With its controlled, explosive jet force you'll put your dream in orbit! It turns "have-nots" into "have its." It turns starters into finishers. It takes underdogs and makes them champions.

The mathematics of high achievement can be stated by simple formula. Begin with a dream. *Divide* the problems and conquer them one by one. *Multiply* the exciting possibilities in your mind. *Subtract* all negative thoughts to get started. *Add* enthusiasm. Your answer will be the attainment of your goal.

Enthusiasm: The Winning Ingredient

Dreamy starters without enthusiasm quickly lose their steam and end up disappointing fizzles, sputtering on the launching pad of life.

A dull knife blade, no longer able to cut; a clouded window, no longer admitting light; a loose guitar string, no longer singing and humming; a sluggish engine, choking and chugging up a muddy hill. That's the picture of a goal-setting, decision-making, problem-confronting dreamer who lacks or loses enthusiasm. Let this same person get an injection of this inspiring power called enthusiasm and the knife is honed to a fresh new edge, slicing and cutting through a jungle of obstacles; the window sparkles again, admitting a fresh new vision of a grand, inspiring view; the string is tuned tight and taut, transforming the dull thud into a vibrant tune.

The sputtering engine breaks into a smooth-running, power-packed machine that leaves the muddy trail behind and turns into a solid expressway.

Take on enthusiasm and the discouraged and defeat-prone personality is reborn as a positive emotionally-charged dynamo. Nothing can stop him now!

Enthusiasm: Don't Block It—Unlock It!

Why, you ask, would anyone deliberately block the flow of an impressive success-producing power such as enthusiasm? Perhaps the primary reason for such unreasonable behavior is fear of a disappointing defeat.

During the height of the Vietnam conflict, an enterprising Texan named Ross Perot loaded a jet plane with gifts and took off for North Vietnam to deliver Christmas packages to the men being held as prisoners of war. His round-the-world flight was dramatized and publicized, and unsuccessful. The North Vietnamese government closed all doors to him.

When Perot returned to the United States he was asked by a newsman, "How do you handle such a disappointing defeat?"

He flashed back, "I'm not defeated. I was raised in the church, school, home, and boy scouts to try." He ended the interview by saying, "I did not fail—to try."

If the fear of dashed hopes restrains your enthusiasm, you can be positive you'll never know the joy of winning. You can be sure of losing if you never try winning. If you never allow yourself to hope, your hopes will never be dashed—they'll just never be born in the first place. If, on the other hand, you allow enthusiasm to build hopes that are crushed, you will learn a lot, try again, and ultimately succeed far beyond anything you ever could have if you had kept your childlike enthusiasm blocked!

Released enthusiasm has immeasurable success-generating power—so much so that it's safe to let it loose! The odds are overwhelming that hopes will not be stopped—they'll be topped!

Enthusiasm-blocking Excuses

Stuffy and musty dignity is another false reason why some people block enthusiasm. Negative thinking dignitaries may say:

"It's corny."

"It's too dramatic."

"It's undignified."

Don't permit these enthusiasm-blocking excuses to keep you so dignified that you become dull. You may be very proper, but not very progressive!

A banker—enthusiastic? Yes. Walter Braunschweiger unlocked enthusiasm and with this persuasive power helped turn the Bank of America from a modestly successful bank into one of the most powerful financial enterprises in the world.

"Possibility Thinking generates enthusiasm and no man has ever calculated the dynamism of this spiritual force," Walter told me as he unfolded the amazing story of this bank that he was serving as vice-president.

"A. P. Gianinni had founded a very successful bank in the state of California and called it Bank of Italy. A couple of us thought a bank with the name Bank of America would be more appealing to the midwesterners who had moved to California. We applied for a charter. I returned home from San Francisco with the charter under my arms, filled with confidence that it would be a success. It was! So much so that Mr. Gianinni wanted the name himself. We negotiated. We merged, and I found myself in a top executive slot.

"One Sunday noon during World War II I got a call from Mr. Gianinni. 'Walter—we know that when the war is over this state will boom. We've got to get ready for the expansion—*now!* We must borrow fifty million dollars immediately!' His decision-making voice was filled with urgency.

"He went on, 'Walter, there's only one place to raise that kind of money—the big New York investment boys. Now Walter,' he paused a minute before he dropped his blockbuster, 'tomorrow at one o'clock they're meeting in New York. You will go there, address them, and sell them on buying this investment opportunity.'"

Braunschweiger was speechless. He knew that such a presentation usually required weeks, perhaps months of research and documentation, to say nothing of the need to carefully mind-condition the men who would be making the decision.

"I knew I couldn't think or say the word impossible, to

the boss. But I did say, 'Pardon me, sir, but how will I get to New York by one o'clock?' I knew that with wartime requirements airline reservations were needed weeks ahead of time. Furthermore, in that prejet age, a flight would take nearly twelve hours.

" 'It's all arranged, Walter. I've called the airline president. They'll have a seat for you on the night flight leaving San Diego. You'll be in New York early in the morning. You can spend this afternoon gathering the vital facts for a formal presentation. You can outline it on the plane. Rehearse the details carefully! Remember that every fact must be spelled out in precise and accurate detail or you'll violate federal law by making erroneous claims for the sale of stocks.' I scrambled to collect the data—our assets, net worth, liabilities, growth statistics, etc. I also made the plane.

"In the early darkness of Monday morning the plane suddenly descended and made an unscheduled stop in a southeastern city. What happened next was a nightmare! I was bumped off to make room for an army general! I watched the dreams of the company disappear as the plane took off and left me—alone in an empty airport.

"Desperately I called the boss. 'Don't worry, Walter—I'll arrange something.' He did. He chartered a special plane. Four hours later I was airborne. But could I make the one o'clock meeting? It was nearly twelve noon when I put down at La Guardia, caught a cab, and feverishly rehearsed the intricacies of this finely detailed and legally accurate presentation. As the cab stopped at the Manhattan address, I was horrified to think that I was still dressed in the suit and shirt I had pulled on the day before and slept in all night. Bristles were sprouting on my face. But I had no time. I dashed in, caught an elevator, and with only moments to spare reached the corridor outside the meeting room. I reached for my written presentation. It was gone! In the hectic rush I had left it in the cab.

" 'Mr. Braunschweiger?' I was being called. What could I do? 'One financial misstatement and we could go to prison,' I thought. I prayed silently and the inspiration came, 'Just be enthusiastic.' But could conservative, unemotional, calculating investment bankers respond to enthusiasm?

" 'How many of you gentlemen have ever been to California?' I began. The dark-suited, unsmiling, frozen faces drew unanimous blanks. I continued, 'Gentlemen, it's a gorgeous state built on sunshine and balmy ocean breezes! Miles of orange groves with their waxen leaves shower the air with fragrant perfume in the winter months. Gentle sunshine falls warm on the skin turning white faces into warm, brown, suntanned smiles. From Iowa, Illinois, Indiana, Minnesota, the tourists come, every frozen January, to bask in this green-flowering garden state, and they spend their money. Finally, when spring thaws the ice in Chicago, they go back, leaving behind millions of dollars, money that never again moves east but stays there in the sunshine to form a growing, swelling, bulging pool of money as momentous as a vast, undeveloped, underground ocean of oil!'

"By this time my enthusiasm was really carrying me along! I did not make a *single precise* statement but concluded: 'Now gentlemen, when the war is over, and it will be soon, the boys who have been stationed in California will come back to live here. The state will mushroom, and Bank of America, chartered to establish branches, will build branches in all of these booming new communities! We will be ready to take in all that money! And I'm giving you the first opportunity to make an investment in what is sure to be one of the world's great banks.' "

His report was finished. What happened next is history. That group of cautious financiers bought the entire stock issue—to the last dollar! Enthusiasm made a fifty million dollar sale! Bank of America's future exploded—then and there!

Enthusiasm: Don't Defuse It—Use It!

"I refuse to hear any more of it lest I unhappily develop a liking for it," was Rimsky-Korsakov's curt comment as he left the premier of Debussy's opera *Pelleas and Melisande.*

"Why resist enthusiasm?"

"If I don't, I might get carried away with it and have to make changes," the tradition-tripped person tells himself.

Man tends to be a caught-in-the-rut nut. We find our nitch and hitch ourselves there. The inclination to resist progress, fight change, and brace ourselves against flashy new ideas explains why enthusiasm is viewed as a danger to be rigidly resisted by Impossibility Thinkers: a bomb to be defused.

"It's never been done this way."

"It's not our company policy."

"It's not in our tradition." With these sweeping, unstudied, negative generalizations, potentially enthusiastic persons become duds!

Responsible Possibility Thinkers, on the other hand, are not antitraditionalists. They instinctively assume that if anything has become a tradition, there must be proven value in it. The last thing a Possibility Thinker does is discard tradition. He rightly, respectfully, and humbly fears he may unwittingly destroy a vital success ingredient in a formula that has been proven by time and experience to be highly satisfactory.

The promoter who goes around looking for traditions to destroy is more likely than not an irresponsible, negative reactionary seeking neurotic attention in a desperate attempt to build a feeble ego.

Why, then, does the mature Possibility Thinker dare to use enthusiasm that threatens to tamper with a tried and true tradition? Because he's confident that there must be a way to keep up with progress and still retain the classical elements of the proven tradition.

"We've done a good job—now let's do it better" is his attitude. So he never *defuses* enthusiasm—he *uses* this creative power as a motivating force to drive himself and his associates to improvement and excellence!

"We've done it well—now let's excel," he tells himself. With this positive attitude he harnesses enthusiasm to assure constant renewal in what would otherwise become a gradually declining and decaying tradition. Traditions, unless constantly renewed by an enthusiasm to excel, update, expand, and improve, are doomed to die.

Don't let anything kill your enthusiasm, including criticism or complaints. Take the positive attitude of the company manager who says, "The complaint department is our quality control department."

Enthusiasm Works Wonders in Education Too!

"A professional obstacle that afflicts too many of our educators is an impulsive negative reaction to enthusiasm." The speaker was a highly successful high school teacher who prefers to remain anonymous. He went on:

> We label all enthusiasm as nothing more than unreliable emotion. We have a hang-up here because we allow the excesses of enthusiasm to blind us to the successes of enthusiasm. So we point out the dangers of 'sloganism'—and fail to point out the positive possibilities of enthusiasm-producing slogans. We assume that emotion is ipso facto anti-intellectual. The result? We make every subliminal effort to educate emotion out of the kids—then we complain because they lack motivation and aren't applying themselves!

Mrs. Walthers is one of the most inspiring teachers in Orange County, California. Her students constantly earn exceptional grades—and have fun doing it.

"What's your secret?" I asked her one Sunday after church.

She smiled, "Well, it's a slight revision of the traditional approach. I start every new class by concentrating the first week on building an enthusiastic Possibility Thinking attitude in my classroom. I know that many of these students have never earned good grades. Their negative self-image is as fixed and firm as a hard chunk of frozen ground in Minnesota—in January. My first-day positive thinking lecture, like the first drops of spring rain, splatters and rolls off. They laugh inside and sometimes I see them sneer openly. The second, third, and fourth lectures—complete with so-called caring slogans—begin to penetrate. By the fifth day I give them their first test. This really thaws them out—and I can begin to plant seed."

"What's the test?" I asked.

"Well, I tell them it's a written test. I assure them—'I'll grade this test. I'll put it in the record book as your very first grade in the course. I will average it in the final grade along with every other major quiz. Write it out. Turn it in next Monday.'" Then she handed me a copy. Here it is:

SIX PRACTICAL STEPS THAT TURN DESIRE INTO EXCELLENT GRADES

"If wishes were horses, beggars would ride." Here are six

steps for you to follow; but first you must sit down and DO the following:

1. Fix it in your mind what definite grade you desire. It is not enough to say, "I want good grades."
2. Determine what you will *give* in return for the excellence in grades. You never get something for nothing. Write down what you will give—put it in writing.
3. Establish a definite time when the excellent grades will be showing up: next quiz, chapter test, report, etc.
4. Write down a plan for carrying out your desire and start *at once*. Put your plan into action immediately whether you are ready or not. Just get started NOW.
5. Write out a statement of the grade you desire, write down the time limit by which you will acquire it; state what you intend to give in return for the excellent grades and describe clearly the plan which you will use to acquire these grades.
6. Read your written statement aloud twice daily—the last thing you do before going to bed and the first thing you do when you get up. Concentrate as you read and believe yourself already possessing this grade.

Take this test yourself! Apply these principles to the dreams and goals you have established for yourself.

Enthusiasm Unlocks Hidden Powers

Nothing militates against enthusiasm more fiercely than Impossibility Thinking. Some of the greatest people in the world today are enthusiasm-igniting Possibility Thinking teachers.

Some years ago, in his book *The Process of Education*, Jerome Bruner challenged the educational community with the startling hypothesis, "Any subject can be taught effectively, in some intellectually honest form to any child at any stage of development." Recent progress by enthusiastic Possibility Thinking teachers working with deaf and blind and handicapped persons is proving him correct!

Although the idea may seem incongruous, many deaf children and adults do learn to enjoy music. Rhythm, intensity, volume, all are teachable.

Deaf children can learn to recognize vibrations of tones in different parts of the body—low tones in the stomach and legs, medium ones in the chest cavity, and high tones in the sinus cavities of the forehead. For the past twenty years G. Von Bekesy, the Nobel laureate psychosomatic researcher, has been carrying out experiments involving the perception of pitch through the skin bypassing the ear entirely producing a feeling equivalent to hearing.

Enthusiasm: You Need It—Feed It

Enthusiasm—what is it? How do you explain this mountain melting power? How can you get it? The word comes from two Greek words *"n"* and *"Theos."* Literally translated they mean "in-God." We speak of such persons as inspired. IN-SPIRITED people! Fill your life with the God Spirit and all kinds of power break forth. In the words of an ancient Hebrew prophet, "The zeal of the Lord will perform it."

Feed your life with a happy positive faith and you'll find yourself:
 1. Uncovering great opportunities;
 2. Discovering beautiful solutions;
 3. Overcoming impossible obstacles;
 4. Unwrapping surprises God has in store for you;
 5. Rolling back the dark clouds, until sunlight breaks through.

That's enthusiasm. How can you get it? How do you feed it? By filling your mind with a positive mental attitude —that's how!

Now find out how to feed your enthusiasm with a positive mental attitude.

9

KEEP CHARGED UP—
WITH A POSITIVE
MENTAL ATTITUDE!

Enthusiasm that never fades. Is it possible? Yes, if you always maintain a positive mental attitude.

Is that realistic? I know it is. Years ago a wise man who wrote the Psalms said in the first psalm that "the blessed man is like a tree planted by rivers of water, bringing forth fruit every season. Its leaf never withers and everything he touches seems to prosper."

Disappointments? Such people don't know the meaning of the word. They speak of "revised appointments." Setbacks? They don't understand—they talk about "regrouping." Depression? It's only the brief sputtering of their engine of enthusiasm, reminding them that the fuel in their inspirational gas tank is running low. They quickly get a refill of positive mental attitudes and away they go again!

Remember: Negative-thinking cynics are swift to label all such persons as "phonies." Many humans have an enormous inclination to suspect the authenticity of what appears to be an amazing claim—until they personally experience it.

If you keep your enthusiasm filled with positive thoughts, you will be amazed at the transformation in your personality. You'll be like a tree planted by rivers of water —the leaves never wither or wilt.

A Vital Lesson in Living

The legend is told of an old man and a little boy who were riding together in a canal that followed a stream through a forest in a strange land. The wise old man picked a leaf out of the water and looked at its veins. Turning to the boy he asked, "Son, what do you know about these trees?"

KEEP CHARGED UP—WITH A MENTAL ATTITUDE! 111

The youngster replied, "Nothing, sir, I have not studied that yet."

The old man said, "Well, son, you have missed twenty-five percent of your life," and he threw the leaf back into the water.

They drifted close to shore and the old man reached down and picked up a glistening wet rock. He rolled it in his hand until it sparkled in the sun. "Son, look at the rock. What do you know about the earth?"

The boy answered, "I am sorry, sir, I have not studied that yet."

The old man threw the rock back into the water and said, "Son, you have missed another twenty-five percent of your life if you do not know about the soil. Now you are missing fifty percent of your life."

They drifted on and dusk fell. The first star appeared in the sky. The old man looked up and said, "Son, look at that star. Do you know its name? What do you know about the heavens?"

The boy sadly replied, "I am sorry, sir; we have not studied that yet, either."

The old man remonstrated, "Son, you do not know the trees; you do not know the soil; you do not know the sky; you are missing seventy-five percent of your life."

Suddenly they heard the roar and rumble of rushing water ahead. The canoe was caught up in a swift current that threw them into fast-moving rapids. The little boy yelled, "It's a waterfall; you must jump! What do you know about swimming?"

The old man answered, "I haven't studied that yet."

The boy quickly retorted, "Then you have lost all of your life."

As all-important as the knowledge of swimming is to the passenger threatened with drowning—so urgent is it for you to develop a positive mental attitude. With it you'll succeed. Without it, your enthusiasm will never survive.

Nine Principles to Build and Keep a Positive Mental Attitude

For years I have observed, studied, and analyzed people who continually hold a positive mental attitude. There are universal principles that operate in their mentality that serve to keep them thinking positively. You can use those principles.

1. *Say something positive to every person you meet everyday no matter what the actual situation may be.* Unrealistic? Yes—if you're an Impossibility Thinker, but very realistic if you're a Possibility Thinker! The enthusiastic person habitually has some good news, a warm greeting, a funny story, an uplifting report, an optimistic prediction! It's a joy to see him coming down the hall. He's good news!

Traveling across the Pacific an announcement was made that at four in the afternoon on a certain day we would pass through the precarious coral reefs alongside Thursday Island, where at the most critical spot the thirty-six-foot-wide ship would have to maneuver through a narrow passage in the reef, which was less than seventy feet wide. At three thirty a crowd gathered on deck as a special Australian pilot was brought aboard to steer us through. As we approached the floating markers, someone remarked, "We're drawing twenty-nine feet of water and the bottom is only thirty-one feet deep." Those words caused anxious tension to spread across the hushed crowd that moments before had been enthusiastic about the beautiful colors of the coral hues in the sea.

A positive thinker responded, "Why that's two feet to spare! We're only going seventeen knots an hour. Besides, the bottom isn't moving. We think nothing of riding in a car at sixty miles an hour hurling toward another vehicle moving at the same speed in the opposite lane. We miss each other by less than two feet in the center dividing line." Suddenly everyone laughed and marveled enthusiastically as our ship made a sharp, skillful circle through the narrow crevice directly below!

Lois Wendell has been my personal secretary for fourteen years. Twelve years ago I received a telephone call from her. Her voice was deeply troubled. "Bob," she faltered a moment before she dropped the shocker, "I just found out—I've got cancer. It's one of the most virulent types," she said.

I rushed to her home. As I parked in front of her house, I thought, "What, in the name of God, could I say to her?"

KEEP CHARGED UP—WITH A MENTAL ATTITUDE! 113

I hoped and prayed God would help me to say the right words. She reminded me years later what I did say:

> You prayed, Bob, and your positive prayer completely turned my thinking from fear to peace of mind. It was a prayer of thanksgiving you prayed, "Oh God we're so thankful today. We're thankful that we discovered this malignancy at an early stage. We're thankful that we live in a country where the finest and best medical help is available. We're thankful that we're living in a day when great advances are being made in cancer treatment. We're thankful that Lois is surrounded by a vast number of friends who can encourage her—a husband, thank you God for him, Christian friends, relatives, neighbors, thank you God for them! Best of all we're thankful, Lord, that Lois has the gift of a beautiful faith. She does not know what the future holds, but she knows Who holds the future! Amen."

I have deliberately chosen such an extreme illustration to prove what I believe with every cell in my being that you can find something positive to say to every person you meet every day in any situation!

The results of this principle when applied regularly will work wonders. It is incredibly easy. It quickly becomes a happy habit. Especially when you relate it to principle number two.

2. *See something positive everyday in every situation.* Look for the good and you'll find it!

A young minister from a tiny church in the west was still dubious about the power of Possibility Thinking, even after attending an Institute at the Garden Grove Community Church. His own ideas for the development of his church were lying buried under a mountain of problems, the most pressing of which was a leaky mimeograph machine! The tight church budget could not include a secretary and the mimeograph machine was long overdue for retirement. One afternoon the young minister was struggling to print church bulletins, and he succeeded in getting ink stains all over his trousers and shirt and wasting twice as much paper as he used. Then he remembered something he had heard at the Institute: *Every problem is an opportunity.*

He tells this story: "I had never really believed this Possibility Thinking. I was still a cynic. It worked, I knew, for Schuller, but it couldn't work for me. Or could it? I recalled hearing a lecture entitled 'It Might Work—Try It!' I decided to try it! I followed the principle—'use your problem to sell a good idea.' So I decided to leave the ink-stained clothes on and wear them that evening when the church board would be meeting."

Several hours later there he was, standing in front of his board saying, "You are wondering, of course, why I wore these soiled clothes to the meeting. Please follow me back into the workroom and I will show you the culprit, the old, leaky mimeograph machine. Gentlemen, not only did I stain my clothes, I wasted six hundred sheets of paper and printed only fifty! The leakage problem is getting worse everyday; and, to compound the problem, the price of mimeograph machines is steadily rising."

The young man's board was made up primarily of businessmen who realized that it was going to cost them more the longer they waited. One elder reached into his hip pocket, pulled out his wallet and said, "Reverend, here is twenty dollars." Another member said, "I'll match that donation." Before the end of the meeting the young minister had collected three hundred dollars, enough to buy a new mimeograph machine. He was overcome with joy and disbelief. Then he thought to himself, Possibility Thinking really works! "Perhaps people would join my church too if I asked them." He started making door-to-door calls, something he had never done in his life. He sold his idea enthusiastically, exuberantly; strangers began to join his church! The enthusiasm spread. By the end of that year sixty new members were added to his church.

"At that rate we'll have six hundred members in ten years, twelve hundred in twenty years, two thousand in thirty years," he reasoned. "Why we'll never be able to handle them on our two acres of land."

He shared this thought with his board. Twelve months later the young minister purchased, with the loyal backing of his membership, twenty acres of land for a new and larger church. Beautiful, exciting plans were on the drawing board for a fantastic church for the twenty-first century!

3. *Habitually think "It might work."* When you see something positive in a situation, do what the young minis-

KEEP CHARGED UP—WITH A MENTAL ATTITUDE! 115

ter did. Think it might work. This feeds the mind with enthusiastic-generating positive thoughts.

A positive-thinking French woman lived in a small house in the Louisiana Bayou country. She loved it. However, she was surrounded by negative-thinking neighbor ladies who grumbled and complained about "living way out here in the lonely, desolate back country."

One day the positive thinker felt she had heard enough. She scolded the disagreeable and disgruntled French settlers saying, "You live on the bayou. The bayou connects to the stream. The stream is connected to the river. The river flows to the gulf. The gulf flows into the ocean. And the ocean touches the shores of the countries of the world. You can go anywhere from where you are."

Knowing that you can go anywhere from where you are, you begin to believe you just might be able to succeed. So you move ahead and actuate principle number four.

4. *Appoint yourself president of your own "Why Not Club."* Ed, a young man who is an outstanding corporate lawyer in Los Angeles and a graduate of Harvard Law School, is married to Vicki, a lovely airline stewardess. He and his wife started asking themselves, "What can we do as Christians to help others?" As Thanksgiving drew close they realized there were hundreds of old people forsaken and abandoned, living in small apartments and rooming houses.

They decided to have a Thanksgiving dinner for those lonely, forgotten people. Ed went to one of the local hotels. He asked the manager whether there was a large convention room available for a dinner for the elderly people on Thanksgiving Day. The answer was very curt and negative. Ed looked at the manager and demanded, *"Why not?"*

After a moment's hesitation the manager said, "All right."

Ed then went to some of the companies with which his corporation had business dealings. He knew they had charity funds available and he asked them for some. The response: "We have a policy against such donations. We cannot give anything at this time. Sorry, Ed." Again, Ed demanded, *"Why not?"* Again he was successful; he got the necessary money. His wife planned the menu, bought turkeys, vegetables, and dessert, and arranged to have the food cooked and delivered hot to the hotel.

As Ed and Vicki sat anxiously in the hotel lobby at eleven thirty on Thanksgiving morning, a thought struck them. What if none of these people accepted the invitations? They had sent out flyers to many small hotels and rooming houses announcing, "Welcome to a Thanksgiving dinner."

They hadn't received any direct replies, and they did not really know how many persons to expect, one or a thousand. The dinner was scheduled for twelve noon. At eleven forty a little old lady, hobbling on a cane, entered the hotel and inquired, "Is this where the dinner is to be held?"

Ed says he was so glad to see her he wanted to jump up and kiss her. There was one guest for sure. Soon others arrived; then more and more. By the time they sat down to dinner, there were three hundred people sharing the spirit of Thanksgiving. What a beautiful time they had.

They decided to found a *"Why Not* Club," appointing themselves president and vice-president, respectively.

This occasion was such an inspiration to Ed and Vicki that they decided to try a similar experiment at Christmas time for the underprivileged children in Watts, a section of Los Angeles. Once again they asked themselves, *"Why not?"*

They made Christmas possible for four hundred children from poverty-stricken homes. They gave them Christmas dinners and gifts, Christmas carols, and the good word about the birth of Jesus Christ.

Why not? if a good idea comes into your mind and you do nothing about it somebody else will. Why not you? Someone else is succeeding. Ask yourself, "If they can do it, why not me?"

Robert Kennedy was fond of saying, "Some men see things as they are and say, 'Why?' I dream things that never were, and say, 'Why not?' "

5. *Activate every positive idea that comes into your mind with the D.I.N.—Do It Now degree.* Never let a positive idea wither on the vine. Catch it. Keep it. Don't let it die in the limbo of inaction. Activate it or it will evaporate.

When positive ideas come into my mind, I write them down immediately. This is extremely important. Keep a prospect sheet for prospective ideas. In front of every good idea, write D.I.N.—Do It Now. D.I.N. before somebody else does and you find you are a Johnny-come-lately.

Sir Alexander Fleming, the Nobel prize-winning Scottish bacteriologist, is remembered as the discoverer of the life-saving antibiotic, penicillin. One morning in his laboratory at the University of London, he observed that the fungus around the bacteria on a culture plate had died. He took a bit of the mold and put it in an empty glass tube for further study. "What impressed me," commented an observer, "was that he immediately acted on his observation. How many of us upon noticing an unusual development only react with 'that's interesting' and do nothing about it!"

Actuate your positive ideas and you plant a seed. Plant a seed and you will begin very naturally to expect that something wonderful will happen!

6. *Practice positive expectations.* Why do some people always seem to be enthusiastic? Because they expect enthusiastic things will happen.

When I find my enthusiasm level dropping below the high energy standard I've set for myself, I can usually pinpoint the trouble—"I'm not expecting anything exciting to happen today!" The solution is simple. Plan something exciting! Come up with an exciting idea and something will begin to happen.

Several years ago, Dr. Norman Vincent Peale and a small group from the Marble Collegiate Church decided at the year's end to test the power of expectations. Each person wrote down his New Year's expectations, put them in an envelope, and sealed it. They agreed to meet and read them aloud at the same time the following year. The results were worthy of note. One man wrote, "In the next year all I can expect is more of the same old miserable life." His expectation came true. A woman listed ten worthy goals she expected to achieve; nine of them came to pass. She admitted that because she expected to achieve these goals she really worked at them. Another man based his expectations on Capricorn, his birth sign, which predicted, "For you it will be a year of difficulty and frustration." He got what he expected! Another woman, also a Capricorn, knew nothing of the astrological predictions. She had a beautiful year. One man in the group died during the year. When the group met again, they opened his envelope. His expectation read, "As none of the men in my family have survived beyond the age of sixty, I expect I may die next year." He did die one month before his sixtieth birthday. Always expect the best and you'll keep your enthusiasm at a healthy high.

7. *Exercise the power of the positive.* Suppose your happy expectations never come to pass? Use this principle: Count your blessings, not your troubles, and with this attitude your spirits remain strong. A letter received from a woman beautifully illustrates the positive "but." I read in part:

> I lost my husband, "but" I still have my children, thank God. Our stocks dropped drastically, "but" I still have my home which is paid for, and that means a lot. My hearing has gotten worse, "but" I can still see to read very well. My son moved out of state, "but" I talk to him once a week for a few minutes on the telephone.

8. *Discipline yourself to become a positive reactionary.* Dr. Norman Vincent Peale was once asked how far he applied positive thinking. Dr. Peale replied, "I apply it to all situations over which I have control." Occasions will arise in your life over which you have no control. Suppose someone close to you is killed in an automobile accident. You had no control over this tragic mishap, "but" *you can control your reaction.* What will this do to you? Misfortune never leaves you where it found you. You will change. You will become better or worse. You make that choice. Become a positive reactionary. Use your head. Make the best of the situation; react positively and instead of multiplying sorrow, compounding the grief, reduce its destructive effect by letting some good come from it.

J. Wallace Hamilton talked about being in the desert between the Arab and Israeli sections. He saw a small boy playing a flute and said, "Come here, lad." Here was a flute that had once been a rifle barrel. An instrument of destruction had been turned into an instrument of music. That is a positive reaction. "Life," someone said, "is ten percent what happens to you and ninety percent *how you react* to what happens to you."

Remember who you are. You are a Possibility Thinker.

The rule of the game is, "A Possibility Thinker never quits!" He doesn't give up—he simply adjusts! He may revise his time schedule. He may scale down the size of his plans. He may rearrange his resources. He will trim his sails—but he doesn't quit! He will regroup, reorganize, reschedule, even retreat, but he will not resign!

"This is the waiting phase," you remind yourself. All things come to the man who never loses patience. "Wait on the Lord, Be of good courage and He will strengthen your heart. Wait I say on the Lord."

9. *Keep your positive emotions charged and recharged.* Fresh enthusiasm is generated by positive emotions. Allow your negative emotions to dominate you and you'll become a discouraged, depressed, or angry and frustrated pessimist. Allow your personality to be guided by positive emotions and enthusiasm will flow through your being. You'll feel in harmony with the universe. Allow negative emotions to enter your mind and you will "feel" negative vibrations that fill you with an inner sense of discord and disharmony. You'll be out of step with the cosmic rhythm of the universe.

You Are a Rhythmic Creature

"Man is essentially a rhythmic being," Dr. Giacobbe writes. "There is rhythm in rest, activity, eating, sleeping, heart beat and harmonial patterns in respiration, breathing, walking. Many organs such as the kidney and liver cannot function for long without the presence of a rhythmic pulsation in the blood system."

Equally important is discovering that your mind as well as your body operates on rhythm. In 1923 professor Hans Berger was the first to demonstrate in his laboratory the presence of rhythm in the human brain. According to the April 1972 issue of *Music Educators Journal,* he found that the waves were constant in frequency and that they were influenced by various physical and mental states. Edward Podolsky in his book *Music Therapy* has said: "Descartes' famous quotation—'I think, therefore I exist'—perhaps should read, 'I rhythm, therefore I exist.' " Furthermore, Edward Podolsky says, "It has now been found that music rhythm has a profound effect on brain rhythm and thus in brain function." Podolsky discovered that the harmonious or disharmonious rhythm of the brain is affected by the stimuli used. He found that music rhythm has a profound effect on brain rhythm and brain rhythm affects brain function.

What does this have to do with enthusiasm? You can determine your brain rhythm by the emotions you feed it. Positive emotions stimulate harmonious rhythm that produces perpetual enthusiasm. Negative thoughts produce negative emotions that cause an internal disharmony in the mind, turning enthusiasm off faster than you can blink an eye. Negative emotions result in a breaking of the internal harmonious rhythm. Tension results. The music stops! Feed positive emotions into your brain and the natural rhythm is resumed. Harmonies are heard once more! You start whistling again.

To keep yourself charged with positive emotions, begin by developing a discriminating sensitivity until you know the difference between a positive or a negative emotion. Here's a list that will help you. Notice that God has engineered the human emotional makeup to offer a "cure" for every "sickness": a positive emotion that we can select to eliminate the negative.

The Positive Emotions	The Negative Emotions
Faith	Worry
Hope	Despair
Love	Anger [Hate]
Trust	Suspicion
Belief	Cynicism
Courage	Fear
Joy	Sorrow
Cheer	Gloom
Security	Anxiety
Confidence	Worry
Admiration	Jealousy
Determination	Resignation
Inspiration	Inflammation
Gratitude	Complaint
Optimism	Pessimism
Friendliness	Hostility
Humor	Tension
Self-respect	Self-condemnation
Meaningfulness	Futility
Freedom	Enslavement

KEEP CHARGED UP—WITH A MENTAL ATTITUDE! 121

Acceptance	Judgmentalism
Complimentariness	Criticism
Ambition	Lethargy
Forgiveness	Guilt
Generosity	Greed
Aspiration	Withdrawal

Next, start running some tests. Which feelings dominate you? Keep the positive emotions stimulated and charged and you will have a positive mental attitude. And in so doing your mind will be in harmony with Cosmic Mind. I call this Higher Power "God." Jesus called the Higher Power "My Father In Heaven." When you have learned to live in harmony with this Rhythm of the Universe, you will be connected to a Spiritual Force that assures ongoing enthusiasm.

You Choose Your Own Emotional Makeup

You do this by selecting the stimuli to which you expose yourself.

1. Check your reading. Does it stimulate the positive or negative emotions?
2. How about the lectures, television programs, and entertainment? Is it positive—or negative stimulation?
3. What are your friends doing to you?
4. How is your religion or the lack of it affecting your emotional makeup?
5. Examine your conversation. Language generates positive or negative vibrations. What kind of a conversationalist are you?

Much has been learned and written about the fact that colors, vocabulary, architecture, art, music, even landscaping send out emotion-stimulating vibrations—positive or negative. Red excites. Green tranquilizes. Certain plants like the cactus are considered by landscape architects to be dramatic, while pines and willows are calming in their mood-producing effect. Some buildings are "cold"—others are "warm."

Your vocabulary—friend or enemy? Most importantly, use of the words you choose in your everyday language will generate negative sensations or positive vibrations. "I lost my father," I said to a friend shortly after dad died. He corrected me: "Never use the word 'lost.' It's negative. He's not 'lost,' and he didn't 'die.' He has 'moved ahead' and you still 'remember' him."

Students of hypnosis know the enormous value of words—as do all public relation experts, diplomats, skillful communicators, and propaganda experts. You can become an expert too.

> Positive Affirmations
> Produce
> Positive Rhythms

To keep a positive, emotionally charged sense of inner harmony, remember this rule: *Never verbalize a negative emotion.* When you feel the onset of a negative emotion, how do you handle it? Never say, "I'm tired, or angry, or hurt." For in so doing you are strengthening and empowering the negative force. You are literally giving in and surrendering your will to an enemy. There's nothing more destructive. By contrast, the positive affirmations abort the negative emotion before it can be born. The only sensible way to fight weeds is to plant thick, healthy grass. The only successful way to destroy a negative emotion is to verbalize a positive statement. You counterattack the invading negative emotion by shooting the positive counterpart. How? By using an affirmation that will release the positive emotion. For instance, you feel badly because you can't quit smoking. You don't verbalize it negatively: "I wish I could quit smoking." By saying this you surrender to, and are overpowered by, this evil force. Instead say: "I enjoy not smoking." "I love the feeling of being free from an enslaving habit." "I love the clean taste in my mouth since I have stopped smoking." By uttering these last true words, you have *started* stopping.

Marriage Troubles

Having emotional trouble in your marriage? You must not trust the negative feelings. So you will not, you dare not,

KEEP CHARGED UP—WITH A MENTAL ATTITUDE!

you must not give life and breath to a negative emotion by blurting out, "I don't love my wife anymore." Instead you affirm, "My feelings for her are changing. I don't understand my new feelings toward her, but this I know, she must have many wonderful qualities or I wouldn't have married her."

Changing Those Around You

Here, too, is the key to success in changing persons around you. I lecture regularly to ministers on how to preach to change people. Don't tell them they're sinners. They'll believe you—and you'll reinforce this self-image! You'll set this negative impression firmly in their minds and their conduct will only prove how right you were. Put a negative image on the film of their subconscious and you can expect a negative picture to develop! Positively affirm that they are the people you wish they were and they will rise to your expectations. Jesus said, "You *are* the salt of the earth." Positive affirmations produce positive expectations, producing positive emotions that produce positive enthusiasm!

Use positive affirmations to succeed in becoming the person you want to be. Affirm: "I am getting slimmer every day." "I am acquiring more knowledge every day." "I am building a stronger financial base every year. I am becoming a more polite and beautiful person every year."

Next read how to use the seven power affirmations to keep you going when it seems like all your hopes, dreams, and reasons for living suddenly appear to collapse around you.

10

NEVER GIVE UP

"The news I have for you is not good," the doctor's face was grim as he faced thirty-two-year-old Pat Nordberg. Her husband, Olie, gripped her hand.

"Go on doctor," she said.

"You have an aneurysm in the most inaccessible part of your brain. Your condition will get no better. You could die anytime. You might be lucky and live if nothing is done about it."

The doctor continued with his cold, factual report:

"Surgery? I'd say there's a ten percent survival possibility—that's all. We would have to lift your brain out of its case. I would actually have to hold it in my hands. We just don't know what that would do to your mental functioning —if you lived through it."

Numb with shock, Olie and Pat walked in a daze to the parking lot—speechless love flowed from heart to heart as they drove home.

"Mommy, Mommy," their five-year-old boy cried as he ran into the waiting, warm embrace of his beautiful mother. It was her son and her husband that made the decision so hard. Should she choose surgery with only a one to ten survival possibility? Should she let things go, hope and pray that the next headache would never come? She remembered the first one some months before. She felt the blood vessel break. She felt the warm liquid flow around her brain under her skull before she passed out.

New X rays were taken. The diagnosis was the same as before. The aneurysm was still there.

"Well, Pat," the doctor said, "it's a big one. If it goes, you're finished." He explained, "An aneurysm is a weak bulge in a blood vessel—we never know when it will blow."

"Why me? What have I done? I've been a good person." Self-pity was mixed with anger as Pat wept alone in her bedroom. Miles away at his office desk, Olie, a brilliant

Harvard Business School graduate, prayed for guidance between telephone calls from customers who were terribly upset about their "enormous problems."

"Seek ye first the Kingdom of God." The words came from nowhere into Pat's mind. Like sweet music that comes on, suddenly sending a soft mood into a room, so the coming of this Bible verse brought divine peace to the red-eyed woman. She now knew beyond a shadow of a doubt what she would do.

She called Olie. "Honey, I am no longer afraid. I know that if I die, God will have someone better than me to love my son and my husband." She paused, and with utter calmness cooly said, "Olie, I'm going to call the doctor and give him my decision—operate."

"Pat's going to have surgery. She's going in tomorrow morning." Pat's next-door neighbor was spreading the word from house to house on their street in Fullerton, California. "Olie's driving her to the hospital on the way to his office—they don't give her much chance of ever coming back alive or with a normal mind, but she says this is the decision God led her to take."

The next morning a pall settled over the kitchens in houses on the street. Children ran to school, husbands went to work, but the women in each house watched their clocks carefully. Olie would be leaving his house at exactly eight o'clock. One neighbor called the others and said, "Let's all step out on our front steps and wave to her as she leaves— and throw a prayer with a smile and a kiss!"

Quietly, cool and calm, Pat entered the car as Olie carried her small overnight suitcase. He opened the garage door and backed out into the street. Pat saw them, her neighbor ladies, all up and down the block, on both sides. She smiled.

In the way a child makes a jack-o-lantern, cutting a doorway out of the top of the pumpkin, so the top of Pat's skull, with saw and drill, was cut out and lifted up—exposing the brain. Reaching into the cranial cavity, the doctor took the young mother's brain in his rubber-gloved hand and removed the weak section of the major blood vessel that was threatening to blow out. Delicately, gently, tenderly—with a touch almost of reverence, he placed the brain back into its place and prepared to close the door on his job.

Like the cut-out top of the jack-o-lantern, the cut-out section of the skull was now put back in place, and a protective metal plate placed over it. The entire skin of the scalp, pealed away for the surgery, could now be rolled back and sewed up. Hair would grow back in time—if she'd live.

To her waiting husband the surgery lasted an eternity. "Was she still alive? Would she ever know him again if she survived? Would she be a vegetable? A maniac? Or childish? Or—"please God, the same Pat I've loved?" These questions raced through his mind as he prayed with a wet face resting down on his open palms.

"Mr. Nordberg?" the doctor's familiar voice brought him to his feet. He faced the somber surgeon, "It's all over now, Olie," the doctor said. "All we can do now is wait—and pray. It may be days before we'll know whether she is going to live and what her condition will be after that." It was the best Olie could hope for.

Her shaven head, wrapped in a white bandage, still and unmoving in the center of the pillow, gave her a deathly appearance. Round the clock, hour after hour, day after day, nurses on duty for twenty-four hours waited, hoping for a sign of consciousness. Would her eyes open? Would her lips move? Would she be able to speak?

On the morning of the fourth day following surgery, the special nurse on duty had turned her back for a moment when she heard a low but clear voice behind her. "Could you bring me some lipstick please, nurse." Whirling, she looked at Pat, whose eyes were open and alert, and the nurse thought, mentally healthy enough to want to look pretty.

If only the sentences had kept coming so clearly. Over the next few weeks Pat's wounded brain was unable to sustain normal speech. Words got mixed up and out of proper sequence. To compound the problem her body was poorly coordinated. Would she ever be able to live a normal life?

Months passed. She was able to ride with her family to church again.

"Pat," a church member stopped her, "I think you could help as a volunteer in the church school for retarded children. We need one adult to watch and observe each teachable child—would you try to help, please?" Pat didn't need to be asked twice! Here was a chance to prove that, although her speech and body movements were not functioning properly, she could still be helpful. The events that now occurred changed her life.

As Pat tells it, "I noticed an eight-year-old girl, Janine, who had no adult volunteer to supervise her. When I asked about her I was told, 'She is only a vegetable. She has no possibility for ever developing. She doesn't even know her mother. She cannot and probably never will walk.' I felt so sorry for her," Pat recalls. "I sat on the floor close to her. All she did was tear paper and flutter her mumbling lips with a finger. It was so sad. I watched her. Then when her eyes looked up at me, I smiled. She stared back at my smile—and a miracle happened! She crawled over and buried her head in my lap and sobbed and sobbed. As I tenderly stroked her back, she wet my dress with her tears. 'Oh, God,' I prayed, 'if love alone will do this to a child what would love plus an education do?' I decided then and there I'd become a child psychologist."

Pat now knew the person she wanted to be. Incredible hurdles and barriers were in the road ahead. Before she could enroll in college she would have to solve the transportation problem The only way to get to classes would be by car. And she had never learned to drive. In her present condition she lacked the physical coordination to pass a driver's test! A bright idea occurred to her. She had heard that Hawaiian dancing was helpful in learning bodily coordination. She decided to take lessons. Two years of continuous and strenuous hula lessons did it. Her body was now in almost perfect condition. She passed her driver's test. Problem number one was now solved.

She enrolled in California State College in Fullerton, California—only to be placed on academic probation. Her wounded mind could not recall what it would read in the textbook. She would read it again! And underline it! And write notes on paper! And memorize the notes! During that early period of college work she averaged only three hours of sleep each night, yet came up with only a C average. But she would not give up. Year after year after year she added units toward a degree.

Thirteen years after surgery she completed her last semester of classroom work, with a high point average! Her speech is now perfect. By trial and error she invented techniques to correct her language problem. Drawing from this experience in overcoming her own aphasic condition, she wrote her master's thesis, "Exercises that Parents of Aphasic Children Can Use to Teach Their Children Self-Improvement."

"Dr. Schuller," said Pat running up to me after a church service one day, "Guess what?—I got it. My master's degree. And I'm going to work with exceptional children in the public schools. God did it. I know it. I felt Him driving me, urging me, pushing me on. My God can do anything."

Pat is now a practicing psychologist.

Undergoers Can Become Overcomers

Insure yourself against crushing defeat and black despair. You can do this by connecting with an unfailing spiritual power source.

The great violinist Paganini was once performing before a very distinguished audience when a string on his violin snapped. The audience was startled but the master musician, unruffled, continued to play on the three remaining strings. Suddenly another string broke. Still Paganini played without hesitation. Then, with a sharp crack a third string snapped. For a brief moment the artist stopped, raised his famous Stradivarius high in one hand and announced, "One string—and Paganini." With furious skill and the matchless discipline of a superb craftsman he finished the selection on the single string with such matchless perfection that the audience gave him a tumultuous ovation.

There may be times in life when one string after another will snap. Grace Anderson's only daughter was killed in an automobile accident. A string snapped. Then her eighteen-year-old son succumbed after a brief illness. Another string had snapped. Finally, her husband died after a heart attack. A third string had snapped.

"I've lost everything, but not my faith," she said to me. And added, "My faith, it is enough for me to carry on." One string is left—her faith in God! You too can be an overcomer when you undergo heartbreak if you have a living faith.

One of my treasured friends and a member of my television congregation is the celebrated entertainer Doris Day. Not many years ago everything seemed to crumble around her when her husband passed away. The man she loved, trusted, leaned on for sustaining her strength and providing affection was gone. As Doris explained:

> I went into my bedroom and cried my eyes out—day after day. One day my son Terry knocked on my door. 'Come in,' I sobbed. He stood there—then spoke. 'How long are you going to keep on crying, Mom? I think it's time for you to get back to work. You've got a lot to give!"
>
> Something happened to me in that moment. It was God. I know it was. For new life came into me! Why should I keep crying? After all, I didn't *lose* him. I am sharing him now with God. Jesus promised—didn't He?

Doris had remembered the lines, "He who lives and believes in me shall never die."

"That's a *promise*," she shouted, her face flashing, laughing through moist eyes.

When Terry closed the bedroom door, Doris got up, determined to tackle an amazing new career on television. "I never go in front of the cameras," she says sincerely, "without silently praying, 'Use me—use me—use me God to lighten some heavy heart somewhere tonight.'"

Faith-Building Affirmations to Give You Holding On Power

You too can find renewal after a serious personal loss or shock. Use positive, emotion-stimulating affirmations to rise up out of sadness, despair, and the concomitant negative emotions that threaten to overwhelm you. Big game hunting calls for big guns. You don't hunt elephants with a sling shot. So use big affirmations for the really rugged times that you may encounter in life. Do it in this fashion: Read the following affirmations aloud; memorize the Bible verses listed under each affirmation; repeat these affirmations and the Bible verses out loud every day and as often as necessary. Keep at it until you find and feel the cloud lift and the sun break through.

1. *I Affirm That I Will Never Be Defeated Because I Will Never Quit*. "Forgetting these things that are behind, I press onto the days that are before me." (Phil. 3:13.)

On the wall of a little hospital in a European village I saw this prayer: "Lord, when we have chosen our way may we never depart from it. When we fall may we rise again. When we face a cross may we see beyond it the crown. Amen."

For two years Mrs. J. Apt, of Orange, California, visited doctors in an effort to get at the root of her illness. Then came the day when a neurologist made a conclusive diagnosis. "You have multiple sclerosis," he said. "There's no doubt. The tests are positive."

As she drove home from the doctor's office that day the young mother felt the need for inner spiritual power as never before. When she reached her house she stopped to pick up her mail and noticed a large tubular package. She opened it. Inside was a large poster. Some weeks before a member of her family had written to our televised "Hour of Power" requesting a copy of the Possibility Thinker's Creed. Here it was. With hands trembling from the inroads of sclerosis, she tore the wrapping open, unfurled the poster, and read aloud:

> "When faced with a mountain
> I will not quit.
> I will keep on striving
> until I
> climb over,
> find a pass through,
> tunnel underneath,
> or simply stay and
> turn the mountain
> into a gold mine!
> With God's help!"

Enormous faith-power surged through her soul and body in that moment. She has never felt defeat or discouragement since that moment. She was convinced, and still is, that God planned that poster to come at the precise time she needed it.

By contrast there is the man who met me after a lecture and said, "You ought to write an *Impossibility Thinker's Creed*."

"What's that?" I asked.

He answered, "My wife believes in one! The slightest problem that comes up really upsets and depresses her." He paused and suggested, "She'd go for a creed that said, 'When faced with a molehill I will certainly make a mountain out of it and I WILL QUIT. I will keep on arguing, complaining, and crying until I get the pity I want, or get sick and tired of feeling sorry for myself.'"

A father was trying to encourage his discouraged son by saying, "Don't give up, don't ever give up!"

The boy replied, "But I can't solve my problems!"

The father told him, "Remember, son, the people who are remembered are those who didn't give up—Robert Fulton didn't give up, Thomas Edison never gave up, Eli Whitney never gave up, and look at Isador McPringle."

The boy said, "Who is Isador McPringle?"

"See," said his father, "you never heard of him. *He gave up.*"

Ask yourself, "Why quit when things are going to change for the better?" They will. Believe that there is a Supreme Cosmic Force in this universe. It's either intelligent—or it's not. It's either loving—or it's not. If this Supreme Cosmic Force is neither intelligent nor loving, then we should indeed have reason to cringe in fear.

All of the great religions believe that man is made in the image of God and that, at heart, man is both a rational and emotional creature, both intelligent and loving, a miniature reflection of God!

Read these great "God is able" Bible verses and build faith to hold onto:

1. "He is able to save completely all who come to God through Him." (Heb. 7:25, Living Translation.)
2. "He is able to help those who are tempted." (Heb. 2:18, RSV.)
3. "He is able to guard until that day what has been entrusted to me." (2 Tim. 1:12, RSV.)
4. "He is able to keep you from falling and slipping away." (Jude 2, Living Translation.)
5. "He is able to do far more abundantly than we ask or think." (Eph. 3:20, RSV.)

Let's Believe in God's Unlimited Ability!

Never quit when, with a God like that, you can tap superspiritual power. This gives you the base of support for all of the remaining affirmations.

2. *I Affirm That God Expects Me to Be Tough-minded and I Am.* "They that do know God shall do great exploits." (Dan. 11:12.)

Heavyweight champion Jack Dempsey said, "To win you have to be able to give and take hard punches." Former Coach Duffy Daugherty of Michigan State University had the same spirit: "When I look for winners, I look for WISHbone, FUNNYbone, BACKbone." Notre Dame's famous football coach, Knute Rockne, had a famous slogan: "When the going gets tough the tough get going."

I have observed that some people are "hold-outs." They never start until they're certain it's safe. Others are "dropouts"—they start but quit when the difficulties pile up. I prefer the "all-outs," those who when faced with mounting troubles give their dream everything they've got. To paraphrase Isaiah, they rise up with wings like eagles. They run and are never weary.

Be prepared to lift a load and walk away with it to the cheers and applause of those who "never dreamed you'd do it."

In the history books he's called Lord Shaftsbury. In his time he was best known as Lord Ashley. Born in 1801, in England, he grew up in aristocratic circles and mingled with relatives and friends who were all of the upper classes, including wealthy factory owners.

A knock at his door was the beginning of his greatness. It was a Christian minister, Reverend G. S. Bull, calling to ask Ashley to do something for the oppressed laborers. His first impulse was to laugh it off. He was no friend of labor.

"But I love God and love all men and therefore must listen," he thought. What he discovered was a shock to him and to all England. Orphan children as young as nine years of age were being sold as virtual slaves to work in the textile mills, their workdays thirteen hours long. His further investigations made him ill.

He faced his wife, Min, and asked her if he should press for legislation to govern such labor conditions. "It will mean that we will offend some of our friends who own factories and mines. It will mean worry, work, and mixing with some people who will be crude and unpleasant."

Lady Ashley answered, "It is your duty, Sir, to Jesus Christ. Forget the consequences. Go forward and never give up."

One year later the Factory Act of 1833 was passed, forbidding children under nine to be employed in factories. The factory owners were hostile, believing their freedom to manage their factories was being restricted by the government. When friends urged Lord Shaftsbury to quit he stubbornly refused. At his iron-willed, unending instigation, a Royal Commission was set up to do what had never been done before: Authority was granted the federal government to enter and investigate what was going on in the mines, underground factories.

The English Parliament was stunned when they heard the Royal Report. Children seven years old, some even of five and six years, were working twelve hours a day in coal mines alongside near-naked girls and women and totally unclothed men. The scene was commonplace, repeated in mine after mine. Faced with these facts, the mine owners admitted they engaged in these practices and Shaftsbury lead in the creation of laws that prohibited the employment of women and children under ten years of age in the mines. He went on to found the Ragged Schools in which the outcast children of London's alleys could live, study, and be loved. God had a plan for his life.

God has a plan for your life too. What's happening to you now is a part of it. So be tough-minded. Brace up. Toughen up. And face your problems with God-given strength.

3. *I Affirm God Has People All Lined Up Ready to Help Me—At the Right Time in the Right Way People I Don't Even Know Will Come to Support Me!* "So be not weary in well-doing for in due season we shall reap if we faint not." (Gal. 6:9.)

I've been astounded at the thousands upon thousands of

people with all sorts of talents, gifts, skills, concerns, and contacts that God brought into my life to make my dream of a great church possible. I often feel I have done nothing but allow my mind to receive God's dream and my mouth to verbalize this dream. God recruited the people to do the job. God has people lined up to fill any and every need.

On October 31, 1942, in the heat of the Second World War, Winston Churchill spoke to a group of dirty, grimy, unheralded, and undistinguished coal miners:

> Some day when children ask, "What did you do to win this inheritance for us, and to make our name so respected among men?" one will say, "I was a fighter pilot"; another will say, "I was in the Submarine Service"; a fourth will say, "None of you could have lived without the convoys and the merchant seamen"; and you in turn will say, with equal pride and with equal right, "We cut the coal."

Yes—they cut the coal to fuel the ships to transport the troops to win the war!

So open your eyes and see the faces of people around you. Open your ears to hear what they are saying. Today, tomorrow, next week, you'll meet someone—someone who is just the person you need! The right person will come along to fill the right place in just the right time. You'll marvel at the way you meet him. You'll know that God set it up!

4. *I Affirm God Is Stronger Than the Strongest.* "I will make you into an iron pillar." (Jer. 1:18.)

Once there was a young man who had a big idea. He felt called by God to become a great leader among men. His heart filled with excitement as he dreamed his lofty dreams. Then discouragement moved in and negatively he cried to God, "O Lord, I am only a child." He knew he would face enormous opposition from the people in power in his land. Kings and priests, no less, would block and knock him. Imagining these obstacles he felt like a broken twig, a slender reed trembling in the stormy wind. To this young man about to quit, God spoke: "Jeremiah! Be not dismayed—I will make you an iron pillar."

God turns softhearted people into solid, iron-pillared individuals. That description fits the character of the Duke of Wellington. This lordly gentleman came to be called the

Iron Duke. He proved to be God's man for God's hour in history. For God is stronger than the strongest.

Ask any student of European history, "Who was the strongest man of the nineteenth century?" Many would think of Napoleon Bonaparte.

When the French Revolution began in 1789 the British rejoiced. Six years later, a young artillery general named Napoleon Bonaparte took command of the chaotic nation. On May 18, 1804, the pope went from Rome to Notre Dame Cathedral to crown Napoleon emperor of France.

With the French victory against the combined armies of Austria and Russia at Auterlitz, on December 2, 1805, William Pitt, England's great prime minister, predicted years of bloodshed. With Russia and Austria defeated, Pitt pointed to a map of Europe hanging on the wall and said, "Roll up that map, we shall not need it these ten years."

By 1813 the tide had turned against the French emperor. Defeated at Leipzig, he was exiled to the island of Elba, but not for long. Two years later, on May 1, 1815, Napoleon sailed to the coast of France with eleven hundred men and started his comeback trail. Eighteen days later and he was once more emperor of France, beginning his hundred day reign. He knew he must win a quick victory over the lowlands, then Austria, to regain full power. It fell to the Duke of Wellington, commander of the English troops, to try to stop the power-mad Corsican.

As dawn broke on Sunday, June 18, 1815, the forces of Napoleon confronted the forces of Wellington in Belgium outside of a small town named Waterloo. Rain fell. The fields were wet and soggy. The first shot rang out at eleven. At three o'clock in the afternoon Napoleon hurled his cavalry at the English right flank.

"The British infantryman is unbeatable," one historian noted, "when he is well commanded." (Just as a simple Christian commanded by Christ is beyond defeat.)

Whenever the fighting was hottest Wellington would ride into it. When a vital section of his line seemed about to cave in and retreat, this iron pillar would ride up and say, "Stand firm, my boys, what will they say of this in England?"

As his officers pleaded for permission to sound retreat,

the Iron Duke bluntly and stubbornly answered, "My plan is simply to stand my ground here to the last man."

It was a victorious, decisive attitude. They held firm. And when Napoleon's Old Guard charged up to hit them at seven o'clock that summer evening, the duke gave the order to attack. The French generals could not believe their eyes as they saw their army smashed in the final defeat! Napoleon met his Waterloo when he ran into a man whom God had made into a pillar of iron!

Try this prayer: "Oh God, make me an iron-pillared person. You will. You are. I feel it. You're in me. I'm strong. Thank you, God. Amen."

5. *I Affirm God Will Turn My Worst Times into My Best Times.* "Quit you like men, Be strong." (1 Cor. 16:13.)

The original Greek word in this verse is *Andrizomai*, which means "Quit acting like a baby—and start acting like a man." Bad times will become your good times when trouble brings the best out of you.

Few leaders of the twentieth century were more courageous and inspiring than was Sir Winston Churchill during the terrible Second World War. Hitler had stormed all over Western Europe. France had fallen, and all of Western Europe, including the Czechs, Poles, Norwegians, Danes, Dutch, and Belgians were under Hitler's heel. America was still uncommitted. The world waited for Hitler's next mad move. Then, the radios around the globe heard Churchill in his historic speech on May 13, 1940, to the House of Commons:

"You ask, 'What is our aim?' I can answer in one word: 'Victory.' Victory at all costs, victory in spite of all terror, victory however long and hard the road may be; for without victory there is no survival. I have nothing to offer you but blood, toil, sweat, and tears."

Two weeks later Mr. Churchill uttered the inspiring words that would weld his nation into an iron pillar:

> Even though large tracts of Europe and many old and famous states have fallen or may fall into the grip of the Gestapo, we shall not flag or fail. We shall go on to the end. We shall fight in France, we shall fight in the seas and oceans, we shall fight with growing confidence and growing strength in the air, we shall defend our Island whatever the

cost may be. We shall fight on the beaches, we shall fight on the landing grounds, we shall fight in the fields, and in the streets, we shall fight in the halls. We shall never surrender.

Two weeks later Churchill once again addressed the Commons and said: "Let us therefore brace ourselves to our duties, and so bear ourselves that, if the British Empire and its Commonwealth lasts a thousand years, men will say, 'This was their finest hour.' "

You, too, can turn your worst times into your best times. Trouble always leads people closer to God—or it drives them farther away. You make the right choice and you turn a tragedy into a triumph.

6. *I affirm I Can Never Fall Away from God's Love.* "Thou therefore endure hardness as a good soldier of Jesus Christ." (2 Tim. 2:13.)

Some friends of mine in the Midwest had two sons born two years apart. I remember well that sad summer morning years ago. The boys were having fun on the lake when their makeshift raft fell apart and the younger son drowned. They were a brave family as they went on. "Life goes on—we must, too," they said. Only two years later their remaining son was killed when he was pinned under a tractor that tipped over in the fields. Some months later the parents visited our church.

"How did you find strength to carry on?" I asked. The mother answered bravely, "A stranger who had heard about our tragedy sent me a letter with a simple affirmation. It said, 'God still loves you.' I repeated that over and over and over and I believe it. And that's enough." Her eyes sparkled. Her husband smiled through glassy eyes. The three of us held hands and prayed. I watched them walk out tall and trusting souls: iron-pillared people!

7. *I Affirm That If I'm Totally Dedicated, I'll Eventually Win.* "Be thou faithful unto death and I [God] will give you the crown. . . . To him that overcometh I will give to eat." (Rev. 2:10-17.)

The *demanding* person runs into resistance.

The *defeated* person runs into indifference.

The *dedicated* person runs into help!

People come to his side—first to see, then to care, finally to help!

Fritz Kreisler, the world famous violinist, was approached backstage by an enthusiastic music fan who cried: "Mr. Kreisler, I'd give my life to play as you do!" "Madame," he quietly replied, "I did."

Only one month after Churchill promised England that their "finest hour was approaching," he said, on July 14, 1940:

> And now it has come to us to stand in the breach and face the worst the tyrant's might and enmity can do. . . . We are fighting by ourselves alone. . . . but we are not fighting for ourselves alone. . . . We await undismayed the impending assault. Perhaps it will come next week. Perhaps it will never come. We must show ourselves equally capable of meeting a sudden violent shock, or what is perhaps a harder test, a prolonged vigil.

Later when his island was being battered by enemy bombs day and night and some frightened leaders were plotting the evacuation of the island, he answered: "Wars are not won by evacuation."

Few words describe Churchill better than the following: "Never give in! Never give in! Never, never, never, never —in nothing great or small, large or petty, never give in except to convictions of honour and good sense!"

If there is one lesson that comes to us clearly out of the Bible it is this: God will not allow His iron-pillared men to be defeated.

The battle Churchill envisioned began around August 6. It was to last into September. Day and night the island was bombed. Hitler's masses of soldiers were poised on the coast ready to invade the island as soon as England's air force was knocked out. (Hitler had a careful plan to deport every male Englishman between the ages of seventeen and forty-five, thus repopulating the island with Germans to forever change that nation!)

Sunday morning, September 15, we know now, the tide of battle turned—by an act of God. At the underground headquarters of Number Eleven Fighter Group in Uxbridge, Middlesex, lights flashed on the huge board on the wall, while on large tables quiet whispering workers moved the models of British and opposing German planes that were now engaged in a decisive battle high above their underground fortifications. Half an hour passed; the British planes would all have to land to refuel after eighty minutes in the air. Churchill was now in the bunkers. He faced Air Vice-Marshal Park: "All planes will soon be on the ground for refueling, we must send up reserve squadrons—or the Luftwaffe will destroy our entire air force while they sit like ducks on the ground for refueling." Then, turning again to the commander of the aerial forces, the prime minister said, "What other reserves have we?"

"None," was the answer.

Then suddenly—was it an act of God?—the discs moved on the plotting tables, showing all the German planes turning, heading eastward, apparently choosing the lull in the battle to refuel their own planes. They could have moved in to wipe out the air force on the ground— and the invasion could have begun!

God knows how much you can take. Never quit! Never give up! The tide will turn. A miracle will happen. There is no hopeless situation until you become a hopeless person! How do you keep hope alive? By tapping the limitless power of prayer.

11
PRAYER +
POSSIBILITY THINKING =
SUCCESS

In the musical play *1776* George Washington asks three profound questions: Is anybody there? Is anybody listening? Does anybody care?

You, too, may ask these questions when you feel disappointed and frustrated. Be assured that the answer to all three questions is an unqualified yes. God is there, God is listening, and God cares about you and your dreams.

The American people will long remember the time in 1970 when Apollo 13 astronauts almost lost their lives. The project began in a routine fashion. The rocket fired perfectly. Everything went well until the spaceship was 205,000 miles from earth when ground control got this message: "We have a problem out here."

At these words people around the world watching on television moved to the edge of their chairs and unashamedly started praying for these brave young men. Millions of people who normally would have been too sophisticated to admit that they ever prayed, freely and openly called on God. An explosion in the fuel supply had put their lives in jeopardy and made it impossible for them to land on the moon. They had to nurse the spaceship back to earth using emergency measures.

When James A. Lovell, Fred W. Haise, and John L. Swigert finally splashed down safely in the Pacific, they were taken by helicopter to the aircraft carrier where the world watched as they stepped out on the deck. A chaplain moved forward. As he offered a prayer of thanks, all three daring young spacemen folded their hands and bowed their heads. *Time* magazine selected for its cover the picture of these three astronauts—heads bowed, hands folded, thanking God for their homecoming. The President of the United States called for a special Sunday of prayer and thanksgiving.

When the near-catastrophe occurred in outer space, and the experts at the manned space center in Houston were trying to figure out how to get the three men back, they needed to plan a simulated correction, reentry, and return. In order to prepare such a plan, they had to have the precise location of Apollo 13 at that moment. To determine the precise location of Apollo 13 far out in space, they did not depend upon the mass of sophisticated electronic equipment. Instead, they asked the astronauts to look out the window and spot a star and take a reading. Ultimately, when the chips were down, Houston Space Center went by the unchanging stars in the heaven!

At the press interview that followed the splashdown, you may remember how "Fuel-nose" Swigert said, "If you are asking if we prayed, I can certainly say we did! We think that the prayers of those around the world helped get us back."

Heavyweight boxing champion Joe Frazier is a great Possibility Thinker who has succeeded through enthusiasm, faith, hard work, and prayer. Frazier is a dedicated and devout Christian who reads his Bible nightly and goes to church regularly. He credits his success as a boxer to his faith in God. As a young boy, Joe dreamed of becoming a boxer. He was inspired by Archie Moore, one of our greatest fighters and one of the outstanding men of our time. Archie Moore had a program called "ABC—Any Boy Can." That program inspired Joe Frazier, but he had no money and he needed a punching bag. Joe Frazier got an old sack and filled it with sand and rags and there was his punching bag.

Frazier believes firmly that success in his profession depends on a willingness to do your "roadwork"—month after month, year after year, hurdle after hurdle. Frazier admits that many times he wanted to stop midway in his daily morning eight-mile runs. He thought nobody would know the difference. "The trouble is," he admitted to himself, "I would be fooling myself and that is the last person I wanted to deceive. Therefore, I go on running the other four miles."

Joe also says, "As important as roadwork is prayer." He

really prayed that night in Tokyo as the United States boxing representative at the 1964 Olympic Games. He won match after match. In the semifinals bout, which he won, he broke the thumb on his left hand. He was depending on his deadly left hook. Now, how could he possibly win the finals?

On the evening of his semifinal ring victory, Frazier went to his hotel room, locked the door, filled a pan with hot water and began soaking his left hand. His thick, swollen left thumb was excruciatingly painful. He said to himself, "This hand is where my power is and my thumb is broken. I am finished. How terrible. I am the only chance right now for the Americans to win the gold medal and I am broken." Then he thought about his childhood. He remembered his dad who did not have a left arm; it was fantastic what his dad could do with just one arm. "If my dad could support a wife and feed thirteen kids," he reflected, "why am I worried about a broken thumb, anyway?" He prayed, and he believed!

The next day when he entered the ring for the final bout against Hans Huber, who was favored to win, Frazier kept his left hand hanging limply at his side. He had an unusual stance. Hopefully, no one would suspect the truth. Earlier, Hans Huber had been warned by his trainers to watch out for Frazier's left hook. Hans noticed Frazier's left hand hanging at his side; he noted his peculiar footwork, but he remembered the stern warning of his handlers and remained at a safe distance from that limp left hand. Huber boxed so cautiously that when the judges' votes were counted, the champion was Joe Frazier, three to two. Sportswriters still speculate what the outcome would have been if Huber had been aware of Frazier's broken left thumb.

Many millions of the most intelligent, learned, and scientific minds living today believe in prayer, practice prayer, and know it works. Among the half-million letters from all parts of the country that I receive each year from viewers of my television program "Hour of Power" are tens of thousands testifying to the reality of God's power in their life as a result of meditation, prayer, and positive tuning in to this intelligent, loving, cosmic power we call God. Here is one example:

I am a small black woman, all of five feet tall, weighing in at ninety-eight pounds. But I feel like a mighty fortress that has weathered many terrible storms.

I witnessed with my own eyes the defiling of my marriage bed, in our home, by my now ex-husband. I was physically attacked for refusing to stop the divorce proceedings after seven years of marriage and eighteen other women. I cried many a night when my children asked, "Where's Daddy?" I worked four jobs this year in order to support my family due to lack of child support. And, along with my own problems I am a teacher in a supposedly ghetto community, in which I see poverty and lack of self-worth among my students. And because I care about these beautiful children (who don't know how beautiful they are) I bring their problems home with me, also.

But the beautiful victory of it all is that with God's help I have taken the legacy of truth, love and life and knowledge, the one gift that my own father gave me, and pressed forever onward.

God has never failed me. I walk with my head lifted to the heavens and *I talk to God twenty-four hours a day.* No matter what the problem, God has enabled me to smile and to give of myself to others less fortunate than I. And believe me, Reverand Schuller, no amount of make-up can create a face that shines with the light of Christ that is everlastingly as beautiful. My daily affirmation is, "Let the light of Christ shine all around me that others may see through the darkness. Let the peace of Christ flow deep within me that others may feel the inmost vibrations of His works." *I also pray at my darkest moments that God will send someone to me to be helped.* For, to give of yourself is truly inner peace.

One of the most amazing statements ever made by a religious teacher was made by Jesus Christ. "And whatever you ask in prayer, you will receive it if you have faith." (Matt. 21:22.) Does this mean that God will give anyone anything he asks for? Of course not. We often don't have the wisdom to know what's best for us.

In a small community in Germany I heard this legend. "Years ago we were troubled with poor harvests. So the villagers prayed, 'Lord, for one year promise us that you will give us exactly what we ask for—sun and rain, when we ask for it.'" According to the legend, God agreed. When villagers called for rain, He sent rain. When they called for sun, He sent sun. Never did the corn grow taller, or the wheat so thick as it did that season. As the harvest time approached, joy turned to sadness when the farmers saw to their shock and dismay that the cornstalks had no corn, the wheat stalks produced no grain, and the leafy fruited trees bore no fruit. "Oh God!" the simple people prayed. "You have failed us." And God replied, "Not so my children. I gave you all that you asked for."

"Then why Lord," they cried, "have we no fruit or kernel or grain?"

"Because," God answered, "you did not ask for the harsh north wind." Without the winds, of course, there was no pollination.

God's Plan

Jesus did not say that God answers all selfish begging, childish, and pitiful pleading. Jesus does say that God answers all prayer. People often pray for utterly materialistic and selfish things. When they receive no miraculous answer to these requests to a deity, they, in doubt and cynicism, say, "See, prayer does not work!" They called it prayer, but God did not call it prayer.

> Prayer Is Not a Scream Nor a Scheme!

Prayer is not a scheme whereby we can move God to our lives, rather it is a spiritual exercise where we draw ourselves to God until we are a part of His plan and His purpose. When we are in harmony with God's universal plan and purpose then we have peace. When we are out of harmony with God and His universal plan and purpose, there will be inner frustration, tension, and conflict. Real prayer is the spiritual exercise of putting our dreams and desires in harmony with God's plan. The following anonymous statement is kept posted on the bulletin board of the Garden Grove Community Church counseling center:

"God has a Plan for me. It is hidden within me, just as the oak is hidden within the acorn, or the rose within the bud. I believe that anything which comes into my life is necessary for my growth. As I give myself more fully to this God-given Plan, it expresses itself more perfectly through me. I can tell when I am in tune with it, for then my mind and heart are filled with a deep inner peace. This peace fills me with a sense of security, with joy, and a desire to do those things that are a part of the Plan; or I am filled with a new patience, a new stillness, that makes it possible for others to unfold the Plan to me.

"This Plan is a perfect part of a larger Plan. It is designed for the good of all and not for me alone. It is a many-sided Plan and reaches out through all the people I meet and all the events of my life; therefore I accept the events and the people who come into my life as instruments for the unfoldment of God's Plan for me.

"God has chosen those He wants me to know, to love and to serve, and we are continually being drawn to one another. I pray that I may become a better instrument to love and to serve and that I may become more worthy to receive the love and services of others, so that together we may more perfectly express God's Plan in our lives.

"I ask the Father within for only those things which are mine. I know that my good will come to me at the right time and in the right way. This Inner knowing frees my mind and heart from all fear, jealousy, anger and resentment. It gives me courage and faith to do those things which I feel are mine to do. When I am in tune with God's plan I am free from greed, passion, impure thoughts and deeds. I no longer look with envy at what others are receiving, nor do I compare myself with them. Therefore, I do not cut myself off from God, the giver of all good things.

"God's gifts to me are many, many times greater than I am now receiving. I pray that I may increase my capacity to receive as well as my ability to give. For I can give only as I receive, and receive only as I give. The gifts of God always bring peace, harmony and joy. So anything which fills me with peace and harmony and does not hurt another is God-given and belongs to me. I believe that any work I feel called upon to do is mine to do. When I am in tune with that which is truly mine, all things work together for the good of all.

"I believe that when I cannot do those things I desire to do, it is because God has closed the door only to open another, a better larger door. If I do not see the door just ahead, it is because I have not seen, heard or obeyed God's guidance. It is then that God uses the trouble or seeming failure which may result to help me face myself and find the inspiration and power to see the right door.

"The real purpose of my life is to find God within my own mind and heart, and to help my fellowmen. His Love, Light and Life will be expressed more perfectly through me, as I keep in touch with the Father. I pray that I may always be led by His unfailing guidance. I thank my Heavenly Father for each experience which helps me to surrender my will to His Will, and brings me closer to Him. For only as I lose myself in the consciousness of His Great Presence can His plan for my life be fulfilled."

What Then Is True Prayer?

True prayer is discovering the inner harmony of mind that results when you are thinking God's thoughts for your life. For example, you are in a boat. You approach the shore. You throw the anchor out until it digs into the sand. You take hold of the anchor rope and pull on it until your boat slides onto the sandy beach. What have you done? You have not moved the shore to the boat. You have moved the boat to the shore.

The whole purpose of prayer is not to give you what you want—when you want it; but to turn you into the kind of person God wanted you to be when He put you on Planet Earth.

How Does God Answer Prayer?

Someone said God answers every prayer in these words: "I love you." Because He loves you He answers every prayer in one of four ways.

1. *When the Conditions Are Not Right, God Says, "No."* Actually, He is even then giving you what you really want because what you really want is what is best for you. What you really want is to be the greatest person you can be! If God says no to your prayer, it is because He has a better way for turning you into a greater person. You can

be sure that God has a dream for you—and a plan to make it come true!

Decision, published by the Billy Graham Evangelistic Association, has saluted the great churches of the world. One of these is The Peoples Church of Toronto, Canada. It is world renowned for sending more missionaries out into the world than any other church. The success story of The Peoples Church is an illustration of how God answers prayer.

In the 1920s, a young minister, Oswald Smith, wanted above all else to become a missionary in another country. He prayed, "God, I want to be a missionary . . . open the door for me."

That was a true prayer. It was not begging, it was not selfish, it was a prayer in which a human soul was trying to become the person God wanted him to be. When Dr. Smith stood before the examining board for the approval of foreign missionaries, he failed the test. He didn't meet their qualifications.

In spite of his efforts, the doors to overseas ministries were shut. One of his reactions to this was to wonder if prayer really works. Here he was offering his life to God and God's answer was clearly "no." Then a brilliant idea came to his mind. "If I can't go, I'll build a church to send others out there." He did. No pastor has ever established a church that has even come close to accomplishing what Oswald Smith's Peoples Church has. In the span of history, we can see how beautifully God answered the desire of Dr. Smith's prayer even when He said no to his precise request. God said no, for God had a bigger and better idea.

One response of God to prayer is NO when the idea is not the best; NO when the idea is absolutely wrong; and when—even though it may help you—it could create problems for someone else. When the conditions are not right, God says NO and

2. *When the Time Is Not Right, God Says, "Slow."*

Nowhere in the entire Bible can you find a Bible verse that says that God will do anything you ask Him to do when you snap your finger. God does not offer an instamatic prayer-answering service.

God maintains control in the area of the *why* and the *when.* If God answers no to your very sincere prayer, and you ask Him why, God will not answer or explain. God doesn't answer your why questions because raising the question means you are not satisfied with the no.

You want to argue and God refuses to be drawn into an argument. He knows that any explanation He might give would not satisfy you.

If God answered every prayer at the snap of your fingers He would become your servant—not your master. God would be working for you instead of you working for God.

God's delays are not God's denials. God's timing is perfect. Patience is needed in prayer. Some people don't suffer from doubt as much as from impatience.

A man said to me, "I have lost faith in prayer." After listening to him I said, "You have not really lost faith in prayer because you are still praying. You haven't lost faith. You simply lost patience."

Longtime members of our church know that we spell the word "faith" . . . P-A-T-I-E-N-C-E.

"O rest in the Lord, wait patiently for Him and He shall give thee my heart's desire. O rest in the Lord, wait patiently, wait patiently for Him."

A sincere prayer offered to God never dies. God doesn't forget about it. It is like a seed planted which will sprout and grow at the right time. If the idea is not right God answers, "No." If the timing is not right God answers, "Slow."

3. *When You Are Not Right God Answers, "Grow."* God answers prayers when people are ready for it. The ambitious person who doesn't rise to the top immediately often prays for success. God answers, "Grow." Power that comes too fast corrupts. If you are not ready, it will spoil you.

Do you have prayers that are not being answered? Maybe *you* have to grow. Do you face an unsolved problem? Perhaps there is something you have to do.

If your mind is infested with negative emotions, you'll be out of rhythm with the God of the universe and your prayer will not be effective.

I once experienced an upsetting situation with a man who was destroying his wife, his son, and the lives of many others. When I tried to help and he turned on me I was reminded of the words of Jesus, "Neither cast ye your pearls before swine, lest they trample them under their feet and turn again and rend you." It was a terrifying experience. I woke in the middle of the night and found my heart filled with negative feelings toward this man. I realized that it was not right for me to have a negative attitude toward another. I am a Christian. I am a follower of Christ. Christ's Spirit must live within me and these negative thoughts surely cannot be at one with the Spirit of Christ.

I prayed to Christ to drain this negative attitude from me. I imagined myself as a car up on a grease rack with a mechanic underneath turning the plug and letting all the dirty old oil pour out of the crankcase. I felt that my body, lying on the bed, was being raised. Christ came beneath me, opened the little valve at the bottom of my heart, turned it, and let all the bitter, negative thoughts drain out. Then He filled it with a new, bright, clean lubricant called love. Prayer has a draining-out power. It can help drain the negativism from your heart.

An aspiring junior executive needed some pastoral counseling. He had his eye on a top position. However, he was passed up and someone else was picked, leaving him bitter, angry, and sick at heart.

In my counseling I suggested the following to him:

> When you get bitter and angry you are not hurting top management. You are only hurting yourself. They go out for lunch and they don't know that you are sitting there stewing inside. Face it. You have been turned down for a promotion. You didn't get the job you felt you deserved and now you are killing yourself inside. Is that going to get you promoted? No. Instead, your negative attitude toward the decision-makers will show. You can't hide it. When they see your reaction it is not going to inspire them to pick you for a top job —not on your life! Your reaction is proof that you have to grow up. When you do, your maturity will show and only then will you get what you want.

Seven years later he did get a top executive spot in that same company.

Is there an opportunity you have been working on and it does not seem to be working out? Perhaps you need to change!

> The self-centered person has
> to grow in unselfishness
> before God says, "GO."

The cautious person must
grow in courage
before God will say, "GO."

The reckless person must
grow in carefulness
before God will say, "GO."

The timid person must
grow in confidence
before God will say, "Go."

The self-belittling person must
grow in self-love
before God will say, "GO."

The dominating person must
grow in sensitivity
before God will say, "GO."

The critical person must
grow in tolerance
before God will say, "GO."

The negative person must
grow in positive attitude
before God will say, "GO."

The power-hungry person must
grow in kindness and gentleness
before God will say, "GO."

The pleasure-seeking person must
grow in compassion for suffering people
before God will say, "GO."

And the God-ignoring soul must
become a God-adoring soul
before God will say, "GO."

Remember: When the idea is not right, God says, "NO!" When the time is not right, God says, "SLOW!" When you are not right, God says, "GROW!"

4. *When Everything Is Right God Says, "GO!"* Then miracles happen! Barriers tumble! Mountains are conquered! Problems disappear and heartaches dissolve!

A hopeless alcoholic is set free! A drug addict is cured! A doubter becomes as a child in his belief! Diseased tissue responds to treatment, and healing begins!

The door to your dream suddenly swings open, and there stands God saying, "GO!"

Ann Kiemel is a beautiful young girl, slight of build, sensitive, and gentle. Standing in front of an audience of big tough men, she can spellbind them when she says in a soft, sweet, feminine voice: "Hello!" She smiles and waits! "My name is Ann Kiemel!" She smiles again, moving her head silently to scan every face.

"I'm a nobody!" She smiles again!

Now she steps forward, her face tightens seriously, and her little voice suddenly mounts up with power as she declares with head up high, "But I'm going to change my world! For I believe in a big God! You watch and see!"

Try praying big, honest, clean, affirmative prayers, and you'll become the person God wants you to be!

12

HERE IS THE PERSON YOU REALLY WANT TO BE

The principles for dynamic successful living have been outlined in this book. Work them and they'll work for you. You can become the person you want to be. You can and will succeed in your vocation, in your personal aspirations, in your life.

As you pursue your grand dreams, never forget the person you really want to be. More vital than success at work or in personal pursuits is the character that you develop in the process. On a very deep level you will seek to be the kind of person that enjoys wholesome self-respect. My final words contain both a promise and a warning. The word "warning" is a positive word. ("Threatening" is its negative counterpart.)

The warning: Don't sell out your self-esteem to succeed. You may gain a profession but lose a personality. Jesus said, "What should it profit a man if he gain the whole world and lose his own soul?"

The promise: There is a way to get ahead without losing your head. You can make your dreams come true and build your sense of self-worth, not destroy it in the process.

You will always want to be the kind of person who can face himself in the mirror unashamed. You not only want to be proud of what you have achieved, but of the way in which you achieved it. You will want self-respect.

Ask yourself, "At the deepest level, what kind of person am I?"

Are You an "I-I" Person?

The "I-I" person finds emotional fulfillment in feeding an insecure ego, sating his selfish pleasures, making sure he gets his own way. When faced with decisions, this kind of person asks questions like:

"What's in it for me?"
"What will I get out of it?"
"Does it fit in with my plans?"

No matter if others like it; no matter if others would be helped; no matter if others are hurting.

He is the nonsharing, noncaring, nonburden-bearing person. Someone is crying? Someone is dying? "Tough! Rough! I've enough problems of my own" is his answer. Instead of "Please let me help you." There's an abundance of evidence to indicate that by nature most people tend to be "I-I" persons.

Some years ago a Detroit, Michigan, bus driver was attacked by a passenger. As the burly assailant beat the driver over the head and broke his arm the other passengers, including a number of men, cowered in their seats. All but seventy-one-year-old Bernice Kulzco who ran up the aisle and pushed and shoved and eventually frightened the bully away. She was punched, she had her glasses knocked off, but she saved the day and was commended by the heads of the bus company and her fellow citizens. The others were good examples of the "I-I" person. The "I-I" attitude affects a person's entire character.

It affects his value system. "I want what I want when I want it the way I want it" sums up his value system in one selfish sentence. "Do your own thing," he says, "I'll do mine."

It molds his emotional life. He soon finds out most people in the world don't sincerely care abut him. Hence he becomes insecure, defensive, oppressive, suspicious, and cynical. He yields to a frenetic pleasure drive in a neurotic effort to escape from facing a self he's not proud of. Or he drives for more power, foolishly believing that power and position will make people look up to him. He mistakenly thinks that he will then truly respect himself too. Too late, or never, does he learn that the "I-I" route never builds self-respect.

It has disastrous effects on his interpersonal relations at every level. Communication becomes a constant problem. For he only "hears" what he wants to hear. He only "listens" when he suspects he can get something out of it. Real communication involves giving and taking. That's dialogue. But the "I-I" person cannot give—so he cannot accept. For accepting is always giving. You have to give your honest humble attention to accept advice, criticism, and suggestions. You have to give a heartfelt concern before you can accept the burdens of others and be able to say, "I care about you."

You have to give your freedom before you can accept involvement in worthy causes. You have to give your time, talent, and treasure before you can really accept responsibility.

One of the greatest lessons we must learn today is that humanity is an organismic unity. We are all in the same boat on Planet Earth. That which hurts others will ultimately hurt us. All people are closely linked on the spacecraft on which we live. An explosion occurs and you hear the bad news or see it on TV. It will distress, anger, worry, or frighten you. It is affecting you! You may eat and be merry, but you'll hear people who will talk about the terrible things that are happening. Mass communication has helped make mankind realize that it is an emotionally organismic unity! Like it or not!

Look magazine (January 1970) summed up our social problems in these words:

> Individualism run amok. It finds voice in the phrase, "I'm getting mine, buddy———you"—"mine" generally meaning money, material good, status and frantic fun. The delivery-truck driver, frustrated by circling the block, parks with his tail end blocking an active lane of traffic. He could have squeezed into a loading zone, but why bother? ("I'm getting mine buddy.") Traffic begins backing up. Two blocks, back, a cross street is jammed; a block down that street, another intersection fills and clogs. What do we do about this needless little problem? "If a truck blocked me," the rugged individualist says, "I'd give him a piece of my mind then, if he didn't move, I'd show him who's boss." "But, sir, you are two blocks back and two blocks over. You don't have the faintest idea who is causing the jam. The three cars nearest the truck just happen to be piloted by women. Your individualism, no matter how rugged, is impotent."
>
> Traffic jams thus reveal how all our lives are intertwined. The drama is played in a thousand ways a hundred thousand times each day. One selfish individual can hijack a plane load of people or take them down in flames.

Are You An "I-It" Person?

"I-it" persons relate primarily to things. They find emotional fulfillment in things.

Want joy? Get something new.
Bored? Go out shopping!
Guilty? Buy a gift!
Fearful? Buy a gun.
Insecure? Build a bigger savings account.
Need to impress people? Cars, clubs, cocktails will do it.
Lonely? Go to a movie, a bar, or a motel.

To such individuals even people become things. Not persons with hopes, feelings, dreams. People are toys to play with, tools to use, trinkets for amusement, treasures to buy, or trash to throw away. Toys, tools, trinkets, treasures, or trash—all things.

1. The "I-it" person is never emotionally satisfied or fulfilled. He finds that things rust out, wear out, wrinkle, grow old, or go out of style. He probably never discovers that things do not feed self-respect, self-esteem on any lasting basis.

2. His attitude also determines his value system. What's the salary? What are the fringe benefits? How much will it cost? These are the questions he asks.

3. He is never truly free, but is forever trapped by the tyranny of things. Paint me, plaster me, patch me, repair, replace, reupholster, or at least rearrange me.

4. He never really loves. "I love you because I *want* you" or "I love you because I *need* you" is the depth of the love relationship of the "I-it" person. He never meets people on a deep level so he never really lives. For Martin Buber wrote, "Meeting is living."

Are You and "I-You" Person?

Those who relate to other people as human beings are "I-you" persons. They see other people as persons who have dreams, desire, hurts, and needs. We all move from the animal to the human level when we become "I-you" persons. This approach will determine your value system and your goals. Decisions will be easy! You ask these questions again: "Will it help?" "Should it be done?" "Is anybody doing anything?" We listen to them and we give of ourselves. There are people like that.

Marine Sergeant M. E. Bingham and his wife, Martha, saw some girls acting "like roughnecks" and "just hanging around" when they moved into their new San Diego home. They invited them into their house to get them off the street and give them some direction. The idea blossomed into a full-fledged club with scores of youths going back to get together and play games.

In Moro, Illinois, Bob Kruse, thirty-one, a part-time farmer, lost parts of both legs when caught in a corn picking machine. His friends not only raised twelve thousand dollars but also harvested his fields and built a concrete sidewalk, driveway, and patio for his house.

In North Bend, Washington, neighbors of a baker who was injured with his wife in an auto accident, manned his shop themselves. Among those helping sell the pastries were a minister and an undertaker.

A Richfield, Minnesota, widow got a new roof for her home. It was installed by the Operation Brotherhood organization, whose members donate several hours each week to an "ability bank" to help people in need.

Once two hundred and forty inmates of Tucker Prison Farm in Pine Bluff, Arkansas, each contributed the one dollar they received as Christmas presents from the state for presents for twenty-five poor children living nearby.

When an "I-I" person or an "I-it" person becomes an "I-you" person—what a change takes place!

The housewife becomes a homemaker.

The sire becomes a father.

The lover becomes a husband.

The lawyer becomes a counselor.

The teacher becomes a person builder.

The doctor becomes a healer of the person.

The truck driver becomes a transporter of vital material.

The salesman becomes a supplier of human need.

The businessman becomes a job-opportunity creator.

The capitalist becomes a builder of a better society through the generating of money.

The religious leader becomes not a propagandizer for sectarian doctrine—but a soul-saver, faith-builder, life-changing inspirer of men!

HERE IS THE PERSON YOU REALLY WANT TO BE

Now here's the vital question! Do you really believe human nature can be changed? Let's test your Possibility Thinking on this. Answer the following questions, true or false:

1. You can't teach an old dog new tricks.
2. Some habits can never be broken.
3. Can "set-in-their-ways" people be changed?
4. A person's character is firmly fixed at age 7? 18? 25? 45? 65?

Can you change human nature? It depends on which Jew you choose to believe:

1. Freud would say, "No, you cannot change people." So he despaired of man. Shortly before he died, Sigmund Freud told Viktor Frankel, "The more I study man the more I despise him."

2. Marx would say, "Yes, change man's economic environment and you eliminate all human ill." So Freudians never make good Marxists.

3. Jesus Christ would say, "No, you cannot permanently change personality only through environment. Put a pear tree in an apple orchard and it's still a pear tree!" And he would also say, "Yes, you can change your life by changing your thinking. Allow the Holy Spirit to come into you and you'll be a new person."

To become an "I-you" person requires a deep spiritual revolution in the normal human heart.

Alexander Pope prayed: "Oh God, make me a better man." His aide said, "It would be easier to make you a new man."

That is possible. St. Paul wrote, "If any man is in Christ he is a new creature." *How* does this happen? "Except a man be born again he cannot enter the Kingdom of Heaven." Jesus said. Don't let the word "converted" scare you. Photosynthesis is the process by which the energy of sunlight is used to convert water or air into plant food. Life is converting food into energy; energy into action; mineral into vegetable, vegetable into animal; animal into man and a selfish man can be converted into a Christ-like person.

One of America's most beloved entertainers is Dick Van Dyke. The secret of his successful personality may have slipped out that night in his Arizona home when, with guests, the game of "Whom-I'd-like-most-to-be" was being played. One person wanted to be Beethoven. Someone else Horowitz. And so it went. When it came Dick's turn he hesitated, and sincerely but shyly explained, "I don't want to sound silly," he admitted, "but I'd like most to be Jesus Christ."

There are millions of human beings living on earth who have accepted Christ into their lives—and they've changed! They're able to love—unselfishly.

What is real love? Here's my definition, "Love is my deciding to make your problem my problem." A true Christian is a really beautiful person.

Some time ago I flew to the Orient on a mission for the United States Air Force. As I put my foot down on earth after nine hours over the Pacific the first one to step forward and shake my hand was a Negro officer with an eagle on each shoulder. He smiled and said, "Dr. Schuller, I am Bill King."

Colonel King was my host on Okinawa and one of the greatest human beings I have ever met in my life. At the conclusion of those few days, when we were driving to the airport for my trip to Japan, I thanked him for his graciousness, his hospitality, and his kindness. He looked at me and said, "Dr. Schuller, I want you to know that we don't give you good treatment to impress you." After a stop at a traffic light he said, "We only treat you well because you are a human being." Then he stopped to allow a group of children to cross the street. After they had crossed the car roared ahead as he said, "And there is only one way to treat a human being and that is first class!"

One colonel I met in Japan told me that he and Bill King had visited some of Bill's relatives in Selma, Alabama, a few years ago. Bill had just been given his eagles and he walked proudly through the streets of his hometown in his uniform. Suddenly two white men came up to him, ripped the eagles off his shoulders and throwing them on the sidewalk said, "You are a fake. No nigger could be a colonel in the American Air Force."

My new friend said, "Bill King just picked them up, smiled and said, 'Well I am not a fraud and I know what you think of me, but I want to tell you something. God loves you and so do I.' At that Bill King walked off. When we were sitting in the car, Bill looked at me with moist eyes, handed me his eagles and said, 'Will you pin them back on, please, Jack?' I pinned them on and was proud to do it!"

How can you become a person that you yourself will be able to live with and like? How can you become ambitious, energetic, constructive, and dynamic, building up your self-respect in the process? By becoming an "I-you" person. And you become an "I-you" person when you become an "I-Him" person.

Become an "I-Him" Person

Relate to Christ. Let His Spirit come into your personality. Like Bill King, you'll love people; you'll climb to the top; and love yourself doing it. Then truly you'll be the person you really want to be.

Inspirational titles
Robert H. Schuller

Robert Schuller has shown millions of people the way to success in business, interpersonal relations, and every other aspect of life through his inspiring messages over the internationally televised program, "The Hour of Power," and through his many books.

___07509-4	MOVE AHEAD WITH POSSIBILITY THINKING	$2.95
___07401-2	PEACE OF MIND THROUGH POSSIBILITY THINKING	$2.95
___07400-4	THE PEAK TO PEEK PRINCIPLE	$2.95
___06499-8	POWER IDEAS FOR A HAPPY FAMILY	$1.95
___06491-2	SELF-LOVE	$2.50
___07417-9	YOU CAN BECOME THE PERSON YOU WANT TO BE	$2.95

Available at your local bookstore or return this form to:

JOVE
Book Mailing Service
P.O. Box 690, Rockville Centre, NY 11571

Please send me the titles checked above. I enclose _____
Include $1.00 for postage and handling if one book is ordered; 50¢ per book for two or more. California, Illinois, New York and Tennessee residents please add sales tax.

NAME _____

ADDRESS _____

CITY _____ STATE/ZIP _____

(allow six weeks for delivery) #SK44